# EXTRAORDINARY ORDINARY Women

### BECAUSE EVERY WOMAN'S STORY DESERVES TO BE SEEN, HEARD, AND CELEBRATED

# Table of Contents

# *Introduction*:
# The Phone Call That Changed Everything

I was standing in my in-laws' living room when my phone rang. The number on the screen was one I had been both hoping and anxiously expecting to see. It was Cecelia, a manager from the IT department at the health system where I worked as a medical assistant (MA). It was 2010, and I had been waiting nervously for this call for days.

"Hello?" I tried to keep the nervous anticipation out of my voice.

"Mandy," Cecelia's voice was warm, professional, with that quiet grace I had come to respect during our interviews. "I have some news I'd like to share with you."

My heart started pounding. I glanced around the living room where my husband's parents were nearby, probably wondering why I looked like I might faint from a phone call. I quietly moved toward the back bedroom, needing privacy for whatever this conversation was about to reveal.

Closing the bedroom door behind me, I sat on the edge of the bed, still hardly daring to hope.

"We've made our decision about the build analyst position," Cecelia continued. "We want to offer you the job."

The words didn't compute at first. IT department? Build analyst? I was a medical assistant with no degree beyond my certificate from vocational school. I had no business in IT.

"Oh my gosh, that's amazing!" I managed to say.

I felt something shift in that moment, not just in my understanding of what was possible for me, but in my recognition of what had been building toward this phone call for years. This wasn't random. This wasn't luck. This was the culmination of something that had been carefully constructed by women who had seen potential in me long before I saw it in myself.

As Cecelia explained the role, the salary increase, the opportunity for growth, I found myself thinking about a conversation in a high school gymnasium more than a decade earlier. The memory of a cheerleading coach named Robin who had refused to let me quit when things got hard swirled in my mind. She'd told me that leadership breeds adversity, and my job was to be present, hold my head high, and stick it out.

I thought about Kathy, the manager who had chosen not to put me on the "do not hire back" list when I left a job without notice as a young, irresponsible twenty-year-old. Who had believed in some future version of me that I couldn't see yet.

I thought about Joanna who had looked at a pregnant girl on welfare and said, "Yes, I'll give you a chance." Who had shown me what it meant to be a woman supported by another woman in a professional setting.

And I thought about Maureen, who had promoted me to "super user" the operational lead that was the 'go to' for the technology questions in the first place, who had championed my skills and created the path that led to this very phone call.

"Mandy? Are you still there?" Cecelia's voice brought me back to the moment.

"Yes," I said, surprising myself with the steadiness in my voice. "Yes, I'm here."

"What do you think?"

What did I think? I thought about how impossibly far this moment was from where my story had begun. I thought about the girl who had bounced between schools, who had lived through family trauma, who had been poor and displaced and judged. I thought about all the times I could have given up, should have given up, would have given up, if not for the women who had refused to let me.

"I think," I said slowly, "that no one will work harder or appreciate this more."

It was a promise I meant with every fiber of my being. And it was a promise born from the understanding that this phone call wasn't just about a job opportunity. It was about the power of women who lift other women while climbing their own mountains.

"Good," Cecelia said, and I could hear the smile in her voice. "Because I believe you're going to do extraordinary things."

After we hung up, I stood there in that living room, holding my phone, and trying to process what had just happened. My life had changed direction in the space of a ten-minute conversation. But as I thought about it more, I realized it hadn't been ten minutes. It had been years in the making.

This book is the story of those years. It's the story of the extraordinary ordinary women who shaped my journey from a traumatized teenager desperate for a fresh start to someone who could receive a life-changing phone call and believe she deserved it.

They were teachers and coaches, managers and colleagues, family members and friends. They were dealing with their own struggles, fighting their own battles, climbing their own mountains. But somehow, in the midst of their own journeys, they found the time and energy to see potential in me, to believe in my future, to refuse to let me settle for less than what they knew I could become.

Some of them appeared in my life for years, becoming mentors and champions who guided me through multiple transitions. Others were there for a season, a moment, a single conversation that changed everything. But each of them left their mark on the woman I became.

They taught me that leadership breeds adversity, and my job is to step forward anyway. They showed me that being lifted by other women doesn't make you weak, it makes you strong enough to lift others in return. They demonstrated that one of the most powerful forces in a woman's life is another woman who believes in her potential and refuses to let her waste it.

5

This is their story as much as it is mine. Because the truth is, none of us becomes who we're meant to be in isolation. We become ourselves in relationships, in community, in the sacred space where one woman sees another woman's potential and decides to nurture it.

These women were ordinary in the most extraordinary way. They were living their own complex, challenging, beautiful lives while somehow finding the capacity to pour into mine. They were fighting their own battles while still having the strength to help me fight mine.

They were mothers and daughters, sisters and friends, bosses and colleagues. They were struggling with their own traumas, their own limitations, their own dreams deferred and hopes rekindled. They were imperfect and human and doing their best with what they had.

And in their ordinariness, they were absolutely extraordinary.

The phone call with Cecelia was a culmination, but it was also a beginning. It was the moment I fully understood that my success was not just my own, it was the result of a carefully woven tapestry of women who had invested in me, believed in me, and lifted me higher than I could have climbed alone.

Now it was my turn to lift.

This book is my attempt to honor them, to name them, to celebrate the ways they shaped my career; but they also helped me form my understanding of what it means to be a woman in the world. It's my love letter to the power of sisterhood, the importance of mentorship, and the sacred responsibility we have to see potential in other women and help them realize it.

But more than that, it's an invitation. An invitation to recognize the extraordinary ordinary women in your own life. An invitation to understand that someone, somewhere, is watching how you move through the world, and your courage might be exactly what they need to find their own.

An invitation to lift while you climb, because that's what extraordinary ordinary women do.

They stand tall. They hold their heads high. And they stick it out.

And in doing so, they change the world, one phone call, one conversation, one act of belief at a time.

# PART 1
# Foundation
## (1997 - 2003)

# CHAPTER
## One

## "She Saw the Leader in Me"

By the time I walked into Wyoming Park High School as a tenth grader, I had already lived several lifetimes worth of chaos. I was sixteen years old and desperate for a fresh start, though I wouldn't have been able to articulate it that way then. All I knew was that I had made a decision: this time was going to be different.

Behind me lay a trail of upheaval that would have broken many kids my age. The Christian school I attended in a church basement turned out to be a cult. The pastor who abused my brother for years before going to jail, landing our family on the evening news. In the aftermath, my mother made a panic-driven move to a small town an hour away hoping for safety, but instead drawing us nearer to my father, and to the chaos of his alcoholism and mental illness. The night he pulled a gun on my brother and uncle forced us to flee our home. Later, I returned from a camping trip to find all my belongings gone, and soon after, we were bouncing between my mom's friend's house and a tiny apartment. Poverty and pain followed us everywhere, marking me as different, as less than, as someone to be picked on.

I had tried to make it work in Whitehall, that small town where we landed after the cult scandal. But the teachers and coaches there looked at me and saw only what I lacked: the right clothes, the stable home, the parents who attended things sober and put-together. They saw a girl who was poor, displaced, and misguided, with a family full of trauma. Their judgment was as heavy as their low expectations, and eventually I couldn't carry both.

So I made a choice that seemed impossible at fourteen: I told my mother I was leaving. I couldn't take the chaos anymore. I was going back to the city, back to my grandmother Freida, back to the only person who had ever loved me unconditionally. And somehow, miraculously, my mother listened. She moved us back, first to an apartment near a local high school Godwin Heights, which was its own kind of culture shock after small-town life, and then, when I said I couldn't handle that either, I transferred to Wyoming Park, another neighboring high school.

Wyoming Park High School was my last chance, though I didn't know it then. What I did know was that I was tired of running. Tired of being the girl who didn't fit, who didn't belong, who couldn't find a way anywhere. I made a quiet promise to myself: I was going to change. I was going to do better.

When tryouts for the cheerleading team were announced, something inside me stirred. I had always been athletic, skilled at gymnastics; but more than that, I had always wanted a chance to lead, even when I didn't understand that particular calling at the time. Maybe it was all those years of instability that made me want to take charge, to create order where there had been none. Or maybe it was simply who I was underneath all the chaos.

My tryout clothes were ill-fitting. We were still poor, still scraping by, but I had talent and that meant I had a chance. When I stepped onto that gymnasium floor, something clicked into place. For the first time in years, I felt like I belonged somewhere.

I made the team.

Robin, my coach, was unlike any adult I had encountered in my academic life. Where other coaches and teachers had seen my circumstances and written me off, Robin saw something else entirely. She saw potential. She saw leadership. She saw a girl worth investing in.

I couldn't have known then that Robin was making a choice every day to see past my secondhand clothes and my complicated family situation to something deeper. I didn't understand that recognizing leadership potential in a traumatized teenager takes a special kind of vision. I just knew that when Coach Robin asked who wanted to volunteer for extra conditioning, I raised my hand. When she needed someone to help run drills, I stepped forward. When she asked for ideas for new routines, I spoke up.

And instead of shutting me down or questioning whether I had the right to take up space, Robin encouraged me. She put me in positions of leadership. She made me captain in my junior year, then again as a senior. Under her guidance, I poured myself into competitive cheerleading with the desperation of someone who finally had something worth fighting for.

Robin couldn't have known that this team, this sport, had become my sanctuary. She couldn't have known that every time she acknowledged my leadership, she was rebuilding something in me that had been torn down again and again. She couldn't have known that Wyoming Park High School was my last stop before I either figured out how to succeed or give up entirely.

But somehow, she must have sensed that I needed more than just coaching. I needed someone to believe in me.

That belief was tested during my junior year. I had to have a difficult conversation with two teammates, sisters, who had made a mistake during our routine. As captain, it was my responsibility to address it and help them understand what went wrong so we could improve. Leadership, I was learning, sometimes meant having hard conversations.

I thought I had handled it well, firm but fair, focused on the team's success rather than personal criticism. But the sisters saw it differently. They were furious that someone like me, someone from my background, with my circumstances, had dared to correct them.

The phone call came that night. Both sisters, tag-teaming their anger, yelled at me through the receiver. Their words were designed to cut deep, and they found their mark. They called me names I won't repeat, questioned my right to be captain, reminded me of everything I didn't have and everything I wasn't. But what hurt most was the underlying message: girls like me didn't get to be leaders. Girls like me should know our place.

I hung up the phone and found my mother. "That's it," I told her, fighting back tears of rage and humiliation. "I'm done. I'm quitting the team."

I meant it. At that moment, all the old patterns kicked in. When things got hard, when people pushed back, when I was reminded of how different I was, I ran. It's what I had always done. It's what had gotten me through cult churches and small-town judgment and culture shock. When I didn't fit, I left.

But my mother, who had watched me try to rebuild myself at Wyoming Park, who had seen me pour my heart into this team, did something unexpected. She called Coach Robin.

The next day, Robin pulled me aside after school before the practice I was planning not to attend. We sat in the empty gymnasium, and she looked at me with those eyes that had always seen more than what was on the surface.

"I won't allow you to quit," she said simply.

I started to protest, to explain about the sisters, about what they had said, about how maybe they were right and I didn't belong in a leadership position after all.

Robin held up her hand. "Leadership breeds adversity," she said. "Not everyone is going to like the hard decisions and communication that happens when you're a leader. That doesn't mean you step down. That doesn't mean you give up your position because of a couple of people's poor reactions and decisions."

She leaned forward, her voice gentle but firm. "You arrive. You hold your head high. And you stick it out."

Those words hit me like a revelation. For the first time in my life, an adult was telling me not to run. Not to shrink. Not to make myself smaller because other people were uncomfortable with my presence, my voice, my leadership.

Robin was telling me I belonged exactly where I was.

"You have leadership gifts," she continued. "Real ones. I've watched you with this team, and you have something special. Don't sacrifice your position because a couple of people can't handle being held accountable."

I sat there in that quiet gym, absorbing words I desperately needed to hear. This was the first time in my life I felt fully embraced for my leadership abilities. Not tolerated. Not questioned. Embraced.

That conversation changed my perspective. Not just my approach to the cheerleading conflict, but my understanding of my own worth. Robin taught me that leadership wasn't about being liked by everyone; it was about doing what was right for the team, the organization, the mission, even when it was difficult.

I didn't quit. I arrived at the next practice with my head high, just as Robin had instructed. I continued to lead, continued to have the hard conversations when necessary, and continued to push our team toward excellence. The sisters and I eventually found our way to a working relationship, but more importantly, I learned that I didn't need their approval to be effective in my role.

By my senior year, I was not only captain again but earned All-Conference honors for competitive cheerleading. The girl who had walked into Wyoming Park desperate for a fresh start had become a recognized leader and athlete.

But the real victory wasn't the accolades. It was the lesson Robin taught me in that empty gymnasium: that my leadership wasn't something to apologize for or hide. It was a gift to be developed and used, regardless of what anyone else thought about my worthiness to wield it.

Robin couldn't have known she was helping to change my life that day. She couldn't have known that her refusal to let me quit cheerleading was really her refusal to let me quit on myself. She couldn't have known that her recognition of my leadership potential would become the foundation upon which I would build every professional success that followed.

She was just a high school cheerleading coach doing her job, seeing potential in her athletes and refusing to let them waste it.

She was ordinary in the most extraordinary way.

Years later, I would find myself in boardrooms and leadership positions, facing criticism and pushback from people who questioned my right to be there. And every time, I would hear Robin's voice: "Leadership breeds adversity. You show up. You hold your head high. And you stick it out."

That sixteen-year-old girl, desperate for a fresh start and a place to belong, had no idea that Robin was teaching her the first lesson in a masterclass on leadership that would span decades. She had no idea that this coach's simple refusal to let her quit would become the blueprint for every time she would need to stand her ground in the years to come.

But Robin knew. Somehow, she always knew.

She saw the leader in me before I saw it in myself. And in seeing it, she made it real.

# CHAPTER
## *Two*

## "The Hard Truth Teller"

I graduated from Wyoming Park High School in May of 1999 by the skin of my teeth. Years of chaos, the cult school, the constant moves, the instability had stripped away any cushion for mistakes. I earned exactly the number of credits required to graduate. Not one more.

Under Robin's quiet belief in me, I managed to find my footing, earning honors in my junior and senior years. But even that couldn't open the doors to any major college. In our house, college wasn't a dream we chased it was a language no one had ever taught me to speak

We were poor. We lived in a sacrificial, blue-collar, low-expectations world where the question wasn't "which college will you attend?" but "what job will you get?" College was for other people's kids, kids whose parents had degrees, kids whose families had money, kids who came from stable homes where education was valued and expected. Not for people with a poverty mindset.

So I watched my best friends pack up for major universities like Michigan State and Western Michigan. I felt left behind. Again. It seemed like everyone else had a clear path forward while I was still figuring out how to take the next step without falling backward.

I had no particular vision for my future. I just knew I had to do *something*, take some step forward, make some kind of progress. That's what prompted me to enroll at Grand Rapids Community College (GRCC). From the beginning, I didn't take it seriously. It felt like a consolation prize, a holding pattern, a place for people like me who didn't have better options.

My cousin, who was a year older than me, was already at GRCC, and we both decided to join the cheerleading team as something to do. An extracurricular activity that might make community college feel more like the "real" college experience our friends were having.

That's how I met Donna.

Donna was different from Robin in subtle but important ways. Where Robin had been nurturing and protective, recognizing my potential when I couldn't see it myself, Donna was direct. She worked at a local healthcare system during the day and coached our team in the evenings. She was fair, kind, and firm, the kind of woman who had carved out her own success and expected others to work for theirs.

But I wasn't working. Not really. I was having fun, maybe too much fun. My grades were slipping, I didn't want to go to class, and I was treating community college like an extended high school experience rather than the educational opportunity it was.

That's when I came up with what I thought was a brilliant alternative plan: medical assistant school. The idea first sparked after I noticed a few commercials about medical assistant programs, and it resonated with me because both my mom and grandma were adult caregivers in the medical field. It seemed like a natural and practical substitute for a traditional college. The National Institute of Technology (NIT) offered a program that would get me into the workforce quickly with a certificate and immediate earning potential. It seemed practical, efficient, and most importantly, it would get me out of the classroom and into

21

the real world where I could start making money and building a life.

I was proud of this plan. It felt mature, responsible, forward-thinking.

I remember the moment I told Donna about my decision. It was after a game, and we were sitting in the bleachers on the stands at the GRCC football field. The field was mostly empty, the sounds of our conversation carrying in the open air. I expected her to congratulate me on finding direction, on having a plan.

Instead, she challenged me in a way I wasn't prepared for.

"Don't quit school," she said, her voice carrying both firmness and pleading. "This is shortsighted. You're only thinking about getting right into a career, but you're not thinking about where you want to be in ten years, twenty years."

She leaned forward, her eyes serious. "I have a degree. I've used it as entry and elevation in the corporate world in healthcare. You're locking yourself into a path that's going to be harder to change later."

I could feel her genuine concern, her investment in my future. This wasn't casual advice from a coach who barely knew me. This was a woman who saw potential in me that I couldn't see in myself, again. But this time, the potential she saw required patience, investment, and faith in a future I couldn't yet imagine.

"You're taking the harder path," she continued. "You think you're taking the easier one, but you're actually making things harder for yourself down the road."

She talked about how her degree had opened doors, created opportunities, given her options. She talked about the difference between a job and a career, between getting by and getting ahead. She talked about the compound effect of education, how learning builds on learning, how credentials create credibility, and how a degree becomes a foundation for everything else you want to build.

I heard what she was saying. But I wasn't listening. Not really.

At nineteen, I was focused on immediate problems: I needed to make money. I needed to feel productive. I needed to start my adult life. College felt abstract, theoretical, like a luxury I couldn't afford financially, or emotionally. I wanted concrete skills, a clear path, and a certificate that would translate directly into a paycheck.

"I'll think about it," I told her, but we both knew I had already made up my mind.

And I had. I dropped out of GRCC and enrolled in the medical assistant program.

Donna's words followed me, though. Even as I threw myself into learning clinical skills, medical terminology, and administrative procedures, I found myself thinking about our conversation in those bleachers. Not with regret, exactly, but with a nagging sense that I had walked away from something important, even if I couldn't name what it was.

Years later, the irony of that moment would become crystal clear.

I was working as a build analyst at the same healthcare system where Donna had worked during my community college years. I had climbed from medical assistant to IT analyst, and I was proud of how far I had come. But I kept hitting walls, opportunities that required a bachelor's degree, leadership positions that were out of reach because of my educational background.

That's when I discovered that Donna was still there. Not only was she still there, but she had become an executive administrative assistant to the president and CEO. She was an incredible force in the organization, wielding influence and respect that came from years of education, experience, and strategic career building.

She had become exactly what she had tried to describe to me in those bleachers: a woman whose degree had served as entry and elevation, who had used education as a foundation for a career that continued to grow and evolve.

Standing in that healthcare system, looking at where Donna had ended up and thinking about the walls I was hitting in my own career, I finally understood what she had been trying to tell me. She hadn't been trying to keep me in a classroom for the sake of education. She had been trying to give me tools for a lifetime of opportunities.

I wonder to this day if she knows how much I thought about that moment. How her words stayed with me even when I didn't follow her advice. How, eventually her prediction about needing a degree would prove so accurate that I would go back to school, first for my bachelor's, then for my master's, because I finally understood what she had seen from the beginning.

Although I would not change my path now, the journey through medical assisting led me to healthcare, which led me to IT, which led me to consulting and beyond. I have so much respect for what Donna was trying to do that day. She was trying to save me from making things harder for myself. She was trying to give me a foundation that would make everything else easier.

She was a woman who had climbed her mountain and was trying to share the map with someone who was determined to find her own way through the wilderness.

That's what extraordinary ordinary women do. They pour into other women even when those women aren't emotionally or mentally ready to receive it. They speak life and wisdom and hard truths because they know it matters. They plant seeds that might not bloom for years, but they plant them anyway because they believe in the potential they see.

Donna taught me something crucial about receiving guidance: sometimes the right advice comes when you are not ready to receive it, and our job is to hold onto it until we're ready to use it. Sometimes the people who care about us most are the ones who tell us what we don't want to hear, not because they want to discourage us, but because they want to prepare us for a future we can't yet see.

She taught me that women who lift other women don't always present as cheerleaders. Sometimes they love us enough to risk our displeasure by telling us we're making harder choices than we need to. Sometimes sisterhood looks like someone caring enough to have a difficult conversation in empty bleachers after a game, speaking truth into our lives even when they know we're not ready to hear it.

And sometimes, years later, when we've finally grown into the wisdom they were trying to share, we realize that their words weren't criticism. They were prophecy. They were love in the form of hard truth. They were an investment in a future version of ourselves that they could see even when we couldn't.

All women who pour into other women should know this: it matters. Even when the person you're speaking to isn't moving in the direction you recommend, even when they seem to ignore your advice, even when they choose the harder path anyway. It matters.

The seeds you plant with your words will grow when the soil of their life is ready. The wisdom you share will be remembered when they need it most. The love you show by telling hard truths will be recognized when they finally understand the difference between what they wanted to hear and what they needed to know.

Thank you, Donna, for caring enough to try. Thank you for seeing potential in a nineteen-year-old who thought she had all the answers. Thank you for speaking life into me even when I wasn't ready to receive it.

And thank you for becoming exactly the woman you were trying to help me become, a woman whose education became elevation, whose foundation became freedom, whose degree became the key to doors I didn't even know existed.

You were right. And it mattered. More than you'll ever know.

# CHAPTER
## Three

## "Grace Under Pressure"

I felt good about my decision to attend the National Institute of Technology for my medical assistant certificate. Despite Donna's concerns echoing in the back of my mind, I felt excited and purposeful in a way I hadn't experienced during my brief time at community college. When I toured the school and learned about the program modules, something clicked. This felt practical and achievable. Most importantly, it felt like mine.

I was a little nervous on the first day of class, that familiar flutter of uncertainty that came with starting something new. But as I looked around the classroom, I felt something I hadn't expected: belonging.

What a beautifully diverse group of women we were. There were adult women with grown children who were starting over, seeking new careers or returning to work after raising families. There were a couple of late teens like me, eighteen and nineteen years old, trying to find our footing in adulthood. And there was everyone in between  women in their twenties, thirties, and forties, all on different timelines of life but united by one common thread: we were all looking to find our way, to give ourselves a chance with this certification.

We were a misfit group in the best possible way. We were women who had taken unconventional paths, who were brave enough to start over, who were willing to invest in themselves even when others might have questioned our choices. We were women who needed to prove to ourselves that we could do something meaningful, something respectable, something that mattered.

And we all came together under the strong, compassionate guidance and love of our teacher, Leah.

Leah was a short, sweet woman with blonde hair and a sweet, round face that always seemed to radiate warmth. She was a wife and mother herself, and that nurturing energy flowed naturally into her teaching style. Everything about her was quiet and fair: her instruction, her correction, her presence in the classroom. When she needed to redirect or correct us, she never raised her voice or made anyone feel small. Instead, her guidance was confident and steady, just as she was.

There was something deeply calming about Leah's approach to teaching. In a program that could have felt high-pressure and intimidating, learning medical terminology, clinical procedures, administrative systems, she created an environment where we felt safe to make mistakes and learn from them. Her patience was extraordinary, and her teaching style made even the most complex concepts feel manageable.

As we moved through various modules of work, we learned more than just medical assisting but about Leah's own journey in healthcare as well. She had walked this path herself, had worked as an MA, had faced the challenges we were preparing for. When different women in our class faced life's adversities like childcare struggles, financial pressures, family crises, self-doubt, Leah was there, cheering us all on, encouraging us, letting us know we mattered and we could do this.

It was her patience and teaching style that made me believe in something I had never fully believed before: I could really do this. And more than that, I could excel at it.

For the first time in my academic life, I found myself genuinely invested in my success. It sounds funny, but I wanted to make Leah proud. There was something about her belief in us, her investment in our success, that made me want to rise to meet her expectations. I took every test, every practical demonstration, every day seriously. I studied harder than I ever had, not because I was afraid of failing, but because I wanted to honor the faith she had placed in me.

Under her guidance, I became a standout student. The girl who had barely graduated high school, who had struggled to take community college seriously, was now excelling in ways that surprised even me. I was engaged, motivated, and discovering capabilities I didn't know I possessed.

Leah saw this transformation happening and nurtured it every step of the way. She celebrated small victories, provided extra support when needed, and never let any of us forget that we were training for something meaningful, caring for people during some of their most vulnerable moments.

At our graduation ceremony, we took an oath to care for patients with compassion and professionalism. I graduated with honors, both academic and attendance, achievements that felt monumental given my history. But what made the moment truly special was seeing Leah there, beaming with pride for each of us.

And then, in a gesture that perfectly captured who she was as a person and a teacher, Leah came to our home to celebrate all that I had achieved.

I can still picture that moment: Leah sitting in our modest living space, genuinely excited about my success, taking time from her own family and responsibilities to honor this milestone with me. It wasn't just a polite appearance; it was a celebration of someone who had poured her heart into seeing me succeed.

That visit meant everything to me. It was validation that what I had accomplished mattered, not just to me but to someone I respected and admired. It was proof that her investment in me had been real, that her belief in my potential had been genuine. Most importantly, it was a win I desperately needed at that time in my life.

This certification wasn't just a piece of paper; it represented something significant. A foot in the door to healthcare. A respectable career path. A place to start building something meaningful. Under Leah's guidance, I had learned the technical skills of medical assisting while also rediscovering my capacity for excellence and my hunger for achievement.

Looking back now, I can see how perfectly Leah embodied everything I needed at that moment in my journey. After years of instability and struggle, after leaving college despite well-meaning advice, I needed someone who would meet me exactly where I was and help me build from there. I needed someone who saw potential in a diverse group of "misfit" women and created an environment where that potential could flourish.

Leah never made me feel like I had taken the wrong path by leaving college. Instead, she helped me make the path I had chosen into something excellent. She taught me that success wasn't about following someone else's blueprint; it was about bringing your best effort to whatever opportunity you chose to pursue.

Her calm grace under pressure became a model I would carry with me throughout my healthcare career. In medical settings, where emergencies happen and tensions run high, I would remember how Leah handled stress, with steady confidence, quiet authority, and unwavering compassion. When I later found myself in leadership positions, I would think about how she balanced being firm with being fair, how she maintained high standards while creating a supportive environment.

But perhaps most importantly, Leah taught me about the power of believing in people. She helped me see what it looked like when someone poured their heart into seeing each student succeed, regardless of their background or previous struggles. She demonstrated that extraordinary teaching was more than having the most advanced techniques or the most prestigious credentials; her belief was the most genuine investment in her students' success.

The foundation she laid during those months at NIT would serve me throughout my entire healthcare career. The clinical skills, the professionalism, the work ethic, the confidence, all of it traced back to those modules of learning under her patient guidance. When I walked into my first job as a medical assistant, I carried with me both technical knowledge and the self-assurance that came from having excelled under the guidance of someone who believed in me completely.

Years later, when I found myself mentoring others, training new employees, or leading teams, I would think about Leah's example. How she celebrated successes, how she handled setbacks, how she made everyone feel valued and capable. She had shown me that lifting others while you climb isn't just about advancing your own career, it's about creating environments where everyone can discover their potential and achieve their own version of excellence.

35

Thank you, Leah, for seeing potential in a misfit group of women and creating space for us to become our best selves. Thank you for your calm grace, your patient teaching, and your unwavering belief that we could do this. Thank you for coming to my home to celebrate my success, for making that achievement feel as important and meaningful as any college graduation.

And thank you for giving me my first real taste of academic excellence, not just the grades and honors, but the deeper satisfaction that comes from working hard for someone who believes in you and discovering that you're capable of more than you ever imagined.

# PART 2
## Young Motherhood
## Finding My Way
## (2003 - 2010)

# CHAPTER
## *Four*

## "The Door That Stayed Open"

After I graduated from NIT with my medical assistant certificate and honors, I worked a couple of short-lived MA positions before landing at a major hospital-owned, family medicine office. This was my first opportunity at a large organization. I had a little experience under my belt by then, but I was still young and very, very green.

I was twenty years old, full of compassion but lacking the professional judgment that comes with experience. My heart was always in the right place, but sometimes that heart superseded common sense in ways that could have gotten me into serious trouble.

I remember one incident that perfectly captured my naivety. There was an elderly lady who came in regularly, and during one of our conversations, she mentioned how hard it was for her to find rides to her appointments. I felt so bad for her, this sweet older woman struggling with transportation, that I did what seemed like the obvious, caring thing to do: I gave her my personal phone number and told her I could give her a ride if she ever needed one.

The next day, Kathy, my manager, pulled me aside. She was a tall, blonde woman with glasses, serious by nature, smart and astute, but with a soft, fun side that appeared from time to time. In her hand was a photocopy of the piece of paper where I had written my phone number for the patient.

"Can we talk?" she said, and I knew immediately I was in trouble.

We sat down, and Kathy explained to me that although my heart was in the right place, this was not the right way to handle the situation. I could connect patients with help lines and ride services, but handing out my personal number put me at risk, put the clinic at risk, and even put the patient at risk.

I was a little confused at the time. I was trying to be nice, trying to help someone who needed it. But Kathy was explaining to me that there were professional boundaries that existed, not to make us less caring, but to protect everyone involved.

It was a gentle but firm lesson in professional judgment, and it was exactly the kind of guidance I needed but didn't know I needed.

I wasn't the best employee overall at the time, either. I was young, and I was living like a young person, going out partying at night, then coming to work the next day with a mostly older crew of women who were my mom's age and older. Sometimes I would slip into the bathroom just to lay down for a few minutes before going back out on the floor, hoping no one would notice I was gone too long or see how tired I was from my night out.

Looking back, I'm amazed Kathy put up with me at all.

What made the situation even more complex was that Kathy had a daughter my age who was off at college. During her breaks, she would work at the clinic, and we became friends. We went to lunch together and chatted during downtime before she would head back to school. I remember feeling somewhat envious of her. Here was a young woman whose mom was a healthcare leader, who seemed to have clear direction and goals, who was off doing great things at

41

college. Meanwhile, I was being a mediocre MA, more focused on having fun than on future plans or goals. At the time, I really had none.

The contrast was stark, and I'm sure it wasn't lost on Kathy.

That's when I met my now-husband. One evening out at a bar, I noticed him, and once we met that night, we became inseparable. He was twenty-three, I was twenty-one, and we were both immature with no major plans for our futures.

On a whim, we decided we were going to move to New York. He had a connection there that might help him get started with what he wanted to do, and I was just young and in love, willing to try any new adventure that presented itself.

So without proper notice, I told my job I was going on a week's vacation. But I just left and never came back.

It was an irresponsible decision that reflected exactly how immature I was at the time. I was thinking with my heart instead of my head, prioritizing romance and adventure over responsibility and professional growth. I left Kathy and the team hanging, left patients who had gotten to know me wondering where I had gone, and abandoned a job that was teaching me valuable lessons about healthcare and professionalism.

New York didn't work out, and we moved to Cleveland with family for a while, trying to find our way. Meanwhile, back at the hospital system, Kathy was left with a decision that would prove to be one of the most impactful choices anyone would ever make regarding my career.

She didn't know what had happened to me. One day I was there, the next day I wasn't. The hospital system asked her at the time if she wanted to put me on the "no hire back" list.

This was standard procedure. When employees abandon their jobs without notice, especially in healthcare where continuity of care matters, managers typically ensure that those employees can never return to the organization. It protects the company from unreliable workers and sends a message about professional expectations.

Any reasonable manager would have said. "Yes. Put her on the list. She's clearly not reliable, not professional, not someone we want to risk hiring again."

But Kathy said no.

I would find out years later, when I met up with Kathy again, about the decision she had made and why she made it. Maybe it was something about my age, the fact that I was her daughter's age and she could see that I was still growing, still figuring things out. Maybe she didn't want to ruin my chance to come back to the hospital system. Maybe she saw something in me that I couldn't see in myself, some potential that was buried under all that childishness and poor decision-making.

Whatever it was that guided her decision, the choice she made kept the door open for my return. It would prove to be the same hospital system that, years later, would give me the opportunity to grow into IT, to become a build analyst, and to transform my entire career.

How impactful that decision was. How could she have known that trusting her spirit, trusting her "knower" as I call it, would mean so much to the direction of my life?

When I returned home years later, I was a different person. I was a mother, more mature, more focused, and ready to take my career seriously.

The reunion with Kathy was emotional for me. Here was the woman who had every reason to write me off, who had every justification for closing that door permanently. Instead, she had chosen to keep it open, to bet on the woman I might become rather than judge me solely on who I was at twenty-one.

"There was something about you," she told me during our conversation. "Maybe it was your age, maybe it was seeing my own daughter at the same stage of life. But I just felt like you deserved a second chance. I felt like you would grow up and come back."

Her faith in my future self, when my present self was so clearly struggling, remains one of the most profound acts of grace I have ever experienced.

Kathy taught me something crucial about leadership and about seeing potential in people. She taught me that sometimes the most extraordinary thing a manager can do is refuse to shut the door on someone's future. She demonstrated that believing in people's capacity for growth and change can literally alter the evolution of their lives.

Her decision also taught me about the power of grace in professional settings. It would have been easier, safer, more conventional, and appropriate to put me on that list. But Kathy chose the harder path, the path that required faith, foresight, patience, and a willingness to be proven wrong if I never did grow up and return.

That experience shaped how I would later approach leadership and management myself. When I encountered young employees who were making poor choices or

45

struggling to find their footing, I would think about Kathy's example.

How do you balance accountability with grace? How do you maintain standards while still believing in people's potential for growth?

The answer, I learned from Kathy, is that sometimes love looks like going against conventional wisdom. Sometimes lifting while you climb means refusing to give up on people who haven't figured out how to lift themselves yet and reaching down a little farther than you planned to.

Kathy couldn't have known that her decision would enable everything that came after, my return to healthcare, my growth into IT, my eventual success in consulting and leadership. She couldn't have predicted that the young woman who abandoned her job for an adventure in New York would someday become someone who could contribute meaningfully to the same organization.

But she trusted something deeper than what she could see at that moment. She trusted potential over performance, future possibility over present behavior, and the woman I might become over the woman I was.

That trust changed everything.

Thank you, Kathy, for seeing something in me that I couldn't see in myself. Thank you for making a choice that defied conventional wisdom and professional protocol. Thank you for keeping faith with a young woman who was still finding her way, even when that young woman didn't deserve such grace.

Thank you for believing in my future self when my present self was so clearly struggling. Your extraordinary act of ordinary leadership—simply refusing to close a door—created space for every opportunity that followed.

You taught me that sometimes the most powerful thing we can do for someone is simply refuse to give up on them. Sometimes lifting while we climb means keeping doors open for people who aren't ready to walk through them yet, trusting that growth and maturity will come in their own time.

Your faith in my potential became a foundation for my faith in others' potential. Your grace became a model for how I try to lead and manage and mentor. Your decision to keep that door open taught me that second chances aren't just about mercy, they're about wisdom, about understanding that people are not fixed in time but capable of remarkable growth and change.

You were extraordinary in the most ordinary way, simply choosing to believe in someone's tomorrow instead of judging them by their today. And that choice, that simple refusal to close a door, changed the entire course of my life.

# CHAPTER
## *Five*

## "She Gave Me a Chance"

The year was 2003, and I was twenty-one years old, pregnant, and desperate. The New York adventure that had started with such hope and romance had collapsed spectacularly,  a story involving near-disasters at underground salsa clubs and body guards escorting us to safety. But that's for another book entirely. My boyfriend (now husband) and I landed in Cleveland, Ohio, and went to live with family in a house owned by his uncle. It was the worst living conditions I had ever seen.

We cleaned it up and tried to make it work, but when I found out I was pregnant with our daughter, that was it. The very moment I knew another life was depending on me, it was time to go back home. To family. To safety.

We returned to my hometown with nothing. No jobs, no stability, and soon our car was repossessed. We were living between my mother's house and my boyfriend's parents' house (now my husband), bouncing between couches and spare rooms, trying to figure out how to build a foundation for the family we were about to become.

I had to apply for welfare, a humbling experience that forced me to confront just how far I had fallen from the young woman who had graduated with honors from medical assistant school. But the welfare program had a work assistance component, and since I was a certified medical assistant, it didn't take long to find opportunities.

The first job was at an ENT (ear, nose, and throat) office, and I was hopeful. I needed work, I needed stability, and I had skills that could contribute. But when the staff found out I was pregnant, their attitude changed immediately. The next day, they let me go, saying they no longer needed help.

I remember my boyfriend's mother (now mother-in-law) dropping me off at work that day, making some comment about how I was at the mercy of her help and her timing for pickup. The combination of losing the job and feeling dependent on others for basic transportation made me more determined than ever to get our own place and create stability for my growing family.

I applied at a local hospital, a competitor of the one I had left so abruptly years before, specifically for a position at the Family Medicine Residency Clinic. That's where I first met Joanna.

She walked into the interview room, a short woman with dark, curly hair, Puerto Rican, with the warmest smile I had encountered in months. There was something immediately welcoming about her presence. Something that made me feel like I could be honest. Like I could be myself.

We went through the basic interview questions and had a good conversation about my experience and qualifications. But I knew I had to address the elephant in the room. I couldn't afford to invest hope in another opportunity only to have it disappear when my pregnancy became obvious.

"I'm pregnant," I told her straight away. "I hope that's not a problem."

Her response was everything I needed to hear and more. "Will you still need to work after the baby comes?" she asked sweetly.

"Oh yes," I said, "I'll be coming back."

And then we both giggled together, and that was it. Just like that, I was welcomed. Not just hired. Welcomed. Into a job, into a team, into what would become a family.

Joanna was more than a manager to me. She was also a mom of a young daughter, and she took me in as a friend and family member. Under her guidance, I was mentored in more ways than just medical assisting. She taught me about professionalism, about healthcare, about balancing work and motherhood, and about believing in myself even when circumstances suggested I had little to believe in.

The office threw a baby shower for me at her house, and I can still feel the love and pride as they supported and encouraged me through the hardest days of trying to get by. These women, my colleagues, my mentors, my chosen family, rallied around a young, pregnant woman who had very little to offer except determination and gratitude.

With the stability of steady employment, we were able to get a car and then an apartment. In October of 2003, two months before my daughter arrived, we moved out on our own for the first time. It felt like a miracle, this young family finally creating its own space, its own foundation.

I worked up until my due date, December 20th, and two days later, my daughter arrived. When I came back to work, I had even more purpose and drive. Motherhood had changed everything about my perspective and priorities, and Joanna continued to be an encourager and confidant as I navigated this new chapter.

She promoted me and championed me to attending physicians working at the clinic who were also looking for medical assistants from time to time. Her belief in my abilities opened doors and created opportunities that extended far beyond our immediate workplace.

It was actually there, after a couple of years, that I was approached to work at an office for a doctor who was an attending resident at that hospital but had a full-time practice in the hospital system I had so discourteously left years before.

By then, I was a different person entirely. A mother, more mature, more focused, more reliable. When the opportunity arose to move to a position with higher pay and new opportunities, I took a chance, I began to bet on myself.

As a young pregnant girl of twenty-one and then a young mom at twenty-two, Johanna was there for me in more ways than a manager typically is. She was like a family member, a supporter, a soft place to land, someone who celebrated love and laughter even in the midst of challenging circumstances.

The women who banded together at that residency clinic gave more than a job; they gave me a community. They taught me what it looked like when women support women, when they create space for someone to grow and thrive even when that person's circumstances aren't ideal.

Today, Joanna is a registered nurse, helping the community through her work and exemplifying what it means to be a mother, wife, colleague, friend, and sister to everyone around her. She represents everything anyone could ask for in a leader and a human being.

I was so blessed to have her during this time of tremendous growth and change. The foundation she helped me build during those years at the residency clinic became the launching pad for everything that followed in my career.

But more than the professional opportunities, Joanna taught me something profound about grace and possibility. She taught me what it looks like when someone sees potential instead of problems, when someone chooses to invest in a person's future rather than judge them by their present circumstances.

When I told her I was pregnant and needed the job, she could have seen risk. She could have seen complications, potential absences, the challenges that come with hiring someone who would need maternity leave soon after starting. Instead, she saw a certified medical assistant who was willing to work hard and commit to come back after her baby was born.

Her simple question "Will you still need to work after the baby comes?" wasn't an interrogation. It was planning and assessing my intentions. It was an assumption that I would be successful, that I would be worth the investment, that this job could become a long-term relationship beneficial to both of us.

That faith in my potential became the foundation for my faith in myself as a working mother, as a professional, as someone worthy of opportunities and advancement.

Joanna taught me that extraordinary leadership often looks very ordinary. It's simply choosing to see the best in people, to create space for them to grow, and to offer support and encouragement along the way. She taught me that lifting while you climb doesn't require grand gestures; it requires consistent kindness, genuine investment in others' success, and the courage to take chances on people who need someone to believe in them.

The baby shower at her house, the promotions and championing, the personal conversations and professional guidance all of it was Joanna living out her values of community, family, and mutual support. Yes, she managed a clinic; but she saw it as her responsibility to create a place where people could belong, grow, and thrive.

Thank you, Johanna, for giving me a chance when I desperately needed one. Thank you for seeing past my circumstances to my potential, for welcoming me not just as an employee but as family. Thank you for showing me what supportive leadership looks like and for creating a community where a young, pregnant woman could find her footing and build a foundation for her future.

Thank you for the laughter and love, for the baby shower and the belief, for treating me like I mattered when I wasn't sure I did. Your extraordinary heart and leadership during that vulnerable time in my life created stability and hope that rippled out to benefit my daughter, my family, and everyone I would have the opportunity to lift in the years to come.

You were extraordinary in the most ordinary way, simply choosing to be kind, to be supportive, and to invest in someone who needed a chance to prove what she could become. That choice changed everything, and I will never forget the women who banded together at that residency clinic and loved on me during that time of tremendous growth and possibility.

# PART 3
## Career Transformation
## (2010 - 2025+)

# CHAPTER
## *Six*

## "The Moment Everything Changed"

After several successful years at the family medicine residency clinic under Joanna's guidance, I decided to take a new opportunity working for attending physicians at a small Family Medicine office within the same health system where I had started years ago the same system where Kathy had made the choice to keep the door open for my future self.

I took the position for two main reasons: better pay and better benefits. I was a young mother looking to continue finding ways to improve our life, and this felt like the right step forward. The health system was large enough to afford opportunities to work in different clinics here and there, which gave me exposure to various workflows and processes.

I had worked in a different family medicine office closer to my home for a while, but I wasn't entirely happy in that position. When the opportunity arose to interview at Kentwood Family Medicine, I felt immediately that this office would be a better fit, especially after meeting the office manager, Maureen.

Maureen was a short woman with dark hair and small features, but she had broad, strong shoulders, a testament to being a horse-and-farm country person her whole life. She had an intense personality and poured everything she had into her job as office manager. This was off-putting to some employees because she was extremely focused on optimizing and tracking all parts and processes in the office. She wanted efficiency, excellence, and measurable results in everything we did.

However, I never minded her approach. In fact, I found myself drawn to her drive and her vision for what the office could become. She allowed me to be part of transformational projects at the office, including me in meetings about optimization decisions and process improvements. For the first time, I was being exposed to the strategic side of healthcare operations, not just the day-to-day clinical tasks.

By late 2009, our clinic had been selected as the first pilot site to launch a new electronic health record system called *Epic*. It was no surprise that Maureen was the first to raise her hand. We were a bustling family medicine practice of seven providers small enough to feel like a family, but busy enough to make the pilot matter. It was the perfect place to test something that would forever change how medicine was practiced.

I remember the day I walked into her office with a request that would change my entire career and along with it, my life.

"Hey Maureen," I said, "if there's an opportunity to be a part of this program as a lead or super user, I would like the chance."

Without hesitation, she agreed. And that's when I became locked in with the analyst build team, working closely with them to understand workflows and build the system that would change how we delivered healthcare.

This is where I met Cecelia and her team, including Ellen and others who would become crucial figures in my professional development. During our collaboration, I found myself asking them questions: "How do you like this position? How did you get to where you are? What does your career path look like?"

During the build phase, my partnership with the analyst team put me in charge of leading dress rehearsals and workflow processes, positioning me perfectly for go-live support. I was standing out to the team in ways I hadn't expected, demonstrating not just technical aptitude but also leadership capabilities and problem-solving skills.

That's when the lead analyst told me something that would plant a seed I had never imagined: "You know that you're basically an analyst at this point in your understanding of build and process, right?"

It was the first time I thought: *Could I really do this? Could I really be an analyst?* Never in my life had I ever thought of that possibility. I was a medical assistant with a certificate from vocational school. The idea of working in IT, of being a build analyst, felt both thrilling and impossible.

But that conversation became the start of a big opportunity in my career and tremendous growth in my life.

Maureen wasn't the kind of woman who was nurturing and soft in the traditional sense. She was a driven woman who pushed me toward potential I didn't know was possible. The timing of her arrival in my path was exactly what I needed. After the soft mentoring of Joanna, I needed the push of a driven leader like Maureen, someone who would give me the opportunity to grow and launch into something entirely new.

I can't quite express properly the gravity of appreciation I feel for that time in my life and what it launched. The impact of so much change that would follow can be traced back to Maureen raising her hand to make us the first pilot site and then granting me the chance to be a super user, the lead in understanding the technology.

I was a young mother at the time, working full time, working for a chance to better our life. This felt like my shot, my way out of poverty and struggle. Even if I was scared, by God, I was going to take it.

Maureen's leadership during that Epic implementation taught me something crucial about seizing opportunities. She didn't just volunteer our office for the pilot program out of obligation; she did it because she saw the long-term value, the competitive advantage, the chance to be at the forefront of healthcare transformation. And when I asked for the chance to be part of it, she didn't hesitate because she saw that same willingness to embrace challenge and change in me.

Her intense focus on optimization and process improvement wasn't just about making the office run better, it was about creating excellence, about never settling for "good enough." Working under her leadership taught me that high standards aren't punitive; they're empowering. They push you to discover capabilities you didn't know you had.

The LEAN projects, the strategic meetings, the Epic implementation. All of it was due to Maureen creating opportunities for me to grow beyond the traditional boundaries of my role.

When the team recognized my capabilities and suggested I could be an analyst, it wasn't just about my technical skills. It was about the foundation Maureen had built by including me in strategic thinking, pushing me to understand not just what we were doing but why we were doing it, and giving me the chance to lead and problem-solve at a higher level.

Her example taught me that extraordinary opportunities often come disguised as extra work, additional responsibility, or the chance to be first to try something new. Most people step back from those opportunities. Maureen gave me the opportunity to step forward.

The transition from medical assistant to IT analyst that began in her office wouldn't have been possible without her willingness to take risks on her team's potential. She could have chosen someone more experienced, someone with a technical background, someone who seemed like a safer bet. Instead, she chose someone who was willing to work hard and learn fast.

That choice changed everything. Not just my career path, but my family's economic future, my understanding of what was possible for someone like me, and my confidence in my ability to learn and adapt and grow.

Thank you, Maureen, for raising your hand when others might have played it safe. Thank you for granting me the opportunity when I asked for it. Thank you for pushing me toward potential I couldn't see and for creating the environment where that potential could flourish.

Thank you for being the kind of leader who doesn't just manage the present but invests in the future, your team's future, the organization's future, and the future of healthcare itself.

And thank you for showing me that sometimes the most extraordinary thing a manager can do is simply say "yes" when someone is brave enough to ask for a chance to grow. That "yes" became the foundation for every opportunity that followed, the moment when everything changed, the launch pad for a career I never could have imagined.

You were the catalyst for a change that rippled out to benefit not just me, but my daughter, my family, and eventually every person I would have the opportunity to mentor and lift in the years to come. That's the true measure of extraordinary leadership the ripple effect of believing in potential and creating opportunities for that potential to flourish.

# CHAPTER
## *Seven*

### "Quiet Grace and Growing Together"

Up until this point in my career, I had been an hourly employee, literally clocking in and out. Every job had been structured around time cards and rigid schedules. When I joined the IT team as a build analyst, I experienced my first salary position, and I was worried about simple things like start time.

I remember calling Cecelia before my first day, asking what time I needed to be there. She didn't give me the hard answer I was used to receiving.

"Most of my team comes in between 8 and 9, the majority by 8:30am," she said casually.

"Umm, okay, thanks," I replied, but inside I was anxious. No one was going to be tracking my time and movement. I was conditioned to be clocked and structured, and this freedom felt unsettling.

I arrived that first morning at 8:00am sharp. Button-down shirt, dress capri pants, flat dress shoes, and nervous as hell. I can still feel all my emotions from that morning as I approached the back stairwell that led up to the second-floor cubes for the analyst team.

As I walked up each step, I felt everything: nervous, excited, grateful, hopeful, proud, scared, and ready to take it all in. This was my shot, my way out of poverty and struggle, my chance to prove that someone without a college degree could excel in the world of technology and healthcare IT.

My first step and challenge was simply to get acclimated and certified. Certification was part of the process, and people you didn't pass didn't get to keep the job. This required several trips to Wisconsin for training and some of the most complicated thought processes and build sessions I had encountered to date.

But I got it. I studied hard, learned from amazing colleagues, took my tests, and passed. With everything on the line, I had become a certified build analyst, ready to hit the ground running.

I remember preparing for one of the biggest demos to date. We had acquired a hospital, and a room full of physicians who were not happy about going on this new system were waiting for our demonstration. I was chosen to lead it. I had tackled a couple small demo's and projects impressing my manager and she felt confident I was ready. I was green and scared, so I prepared fiercely, knowing that this presentation could make or break my credibility with the team.

In the back of the room during the demo were my manager, Cecelia, and the lead analyst at the time, Ellen. After what seemed like the longest demonstration of my life, they both approached me.

"That was the best demonstration I have ever seen," Ellen said.

I was totally shocked. *Really? Me? The best?* Each time Cecelia gave me an opportunity, I had the support, encouragement, and boots-on-the-ground mentorship from Ellen to help me succeed.

Cecelia would have regular touch-bases with me. She was a tall, elegant woman with dark brown hair, slender, with a beautiful, kind face. She never raised her voice, never had to, and handled serious, hard matters with such poise and grace. Every time she promoted me, I told her again and again, as I had the day she hired me: "No one will work harder or appreciate this more than me." I truly meant it.

As I climbed the analyst ladder — Analyst 1, 2, 3, and Lead — I learned that I had so much to offer the customers and people around me. I was good at what I did and was growing into a strong leader. And through it all, Ellen was my constant support and guide.

Ellen had a similar background to mine. Neither of us had college degrees, but our experience in healthcare support had brought us to these roles. Although she was more polished than I was, she became my rock and support both personally and professionally.

So when it was time to grow in our careers, we both recognized we would only go so far without our degrees. I remember the phone call from HR when I didn't get a position I was qualified for. They said it just came down to me not having my degree.

I hung up the phone with them and immediately picked up the phone to GRCC to enroll. Shortly after, Ellen did the same.

We would work twelve- to fourteen-hour days implementing software, then drive downtown for classes at night, cutting open sheep brains in the science lab, and be back to work in the morning. We were both starting from ground zero academically, but we walked through it together. Navigating marriages, children, career dynamics and school, hand in hand, every car ride, every conversation was the glue keeping us focused on the ultimate goal.

Study sessions on lunch breaks, commiserating over tests and discussion boards while being professional leaders consumed our days. By that time, I was a lead and she was a supervisor, soon to be manager. We were juggling full-time demanding careers with full-time college coursework, supporting each other every step of the way.

During that time, my grandmother, one foundational character in my life, whom we'll learn more about later, passed away. She was diagnosed with cancer in October of 2015 and died less than 30 days later. I was exhausted, caring for her, working full-time, going to school, and managing my family responsibilities.

Ellen would stop by the hospital just to check on me. I would be studying in the waiting room between visits, and she would bring food and drinks, offering quiet support when I needed it most.

It would be an ironic twist of fate that the day she offered me a promotion to supervisor of the implementation team was at the exact time my grandmother took her last breath. It was poetic, the juxtaposition of that moment in my life: profound loss and professional advancement happening simultaneously. Ellen's personal and professional support helped to carry me through it all.

The day I took a new opportunity after getting my degree at another hospital system, I will never forget: we sat out on the corner and cried together.

"My only hope is that I did right by you," she said through her tears.

And you did, Ellen. You did right by me and every other person you have led.

I'm indebted to the way she carried my spirit, pushed my potential, and told me how amazing I was before I could believe it myself. Cecelia's quiet grace and strong leadership helped us both become the women we are today.

Even though I can't talk to either of them as often as I would like, there is a bond there. The hours spent in the trenches, hours at school, hours implementing software, late hours have created a life connection that cannot be broken.

Cecelia taught me what leadership could look like when it's rooted in quiet confidence rather than loud authority. She never needed to raise her voice because her competence, her fairness, and her investment in her team's success spoke louder than any dramatic gesture could. She promoted me swiftly through the ranks because she saw consistent performance, and she told me so.

"You are consistently standing out," she would remind me during our regular check-ins. Those words meant everything to someone who had always worried about not being good enough, not having the right credentials, not belonging in professional spaces.

Her elegant way of handling high pressure situations, her poise during difficult conversations, her ability to see potential and invest in it all of this became a model for how I would later approach my own leadership roles. She taught me that extraordinary leadership often looks very ordinary on the surface: consistent recognition, fair treatment, clear communication, and genuine investment in people's growth.

Ellen taught me what partnership looks like in professional growth. She could have seen me as competition, another person climbing the same ladder, seeking the same promotions. Instead, she chose collaboration. She chose mutual support. She chose to celebrate my successes as if they were her own.

When we both realized we needed degrees to advance, we didn't compete over who would get there first or who would do better. We studied together, supported each other, and made the journey less lonely by walking it side by side. Ellen taught me that lifting while you climb does not just mean helping people below you; sometimes it means linking arms with someone at your level and helping each other reach the next rung together.

The fact that she was there during my grandmother's illness, bringing food to the hospital, checking on me in the waiting room, that went far beyond professional obligation. That was sisterhood. That was love in action.

And the timing of her job offer on the day my grandmother died wasn't just coincidence. It was Ellen who understood that life continues even in the midst of grief, and that sometimes the best way to honor someone we've lost is to keep growing, keep accepting new challenges, keep becoming the person they believed we could be.

Together, Cecelia and Ellen created the foundation for everything that would follow in my career. Both women proved that believing in someone's potential and investing in their success creates ripple effects that extend far beyond any single job or promotion.

Thank you, Cecelia, for your quiet grace, for promoting me swiftly when I proved myself, for never making me feel less than because I lacked a degree, for showing me what elegant leadership looks like under pressure.

Thank you, Ellen, for walking beside me rather than ahead of or behind me, for studying sheep brains after 14-hour workdays, for bringing food to hospital waiting rooms, for crying with me when I left, for showing me what partnership in professional growth really means.

Both of you were extraordinary in the most ordinary way, doing your jobs with excellence, treating people with dignity, investing in potential, and lifting while you climbed. The bond we forged through those intense years of working and learning and growing together cannot be broken, and the foundation you helped me build enabled everything that came after.

You taught me that some of the most important relationships in our lives are forged not in moments of celebration, but in the trenches, late nights implementing software, early mornings studying for exams, quiet moments in hospital hallways, tearful goodbyes on street corners.

That's where real sisterhood is born. That's where extraordinary ordinary women leave their mark on each other's lives forever.

# CHAPTER
## Eight

### "She Fought Her Own Battles
### While Lifting Me"

Leaving Ellen and the position where I had grown so much wasn't easy, but I knew it was time to move on. By then, I had obtained my bachelor's degree and was close to receiving my master's degree. I was looking for job opportunities to diversify my experience, and I had learned that I could take a chance on myself. I was ready to do just that.

I found a position titled "Client Services Consultant" for another hospital system. There was a local chapter, but it was the second-largest Catholic health system in the United States. The scope and scale of the opportunity felt both exciting and intimidating.

I had my interview with Stephanie and liked her right away. She asked me great questions about strategy, organization, and vision  higher-level questions for a higher-level position. I could see she was serious but kind, a no-nonsense woman with a sense of style. Stephanie was a force, and I respected her immediately.

During the interview, the topic of salary expectations came up, as it always does. I let her know my thoughts, and she simply said, "Do some research. Know your worth and how to negotiate."

So before I officially responded to the recruiter, I did just that. This was the first time I asked for a six-figure salary. She had subtly ensured I knew my worth before I even walked through the doors.

I remember this moment clearly. I was sitting in the parking lot outside my daughter's volleyball practice when I got the phone call. I was offered the job and accepted it along with the six-figure salary. I hung up the phone and cried.

My first day, I dressed in a suit jacket and carried my red leather briefcase (I had gotten it secondhand from a former colleague). I was overwhelmed when I walked around the corner to see my workspace. I had a full office with an official nameplate and a table and chairs in the corner for meetings. I was once again so scared, so excited, and ready to tackle whatever came next.

I clearly remember how unsure I was when I had to interact with vendors, legal teams, and other stakeholders. I had only worked with Epic before, and now I was responsible for a portfolio of IT projects ranging from large new construction initiatives to cafeteria POS software to cardiology surgical IT upgrades. I was learning so much, and Stephanie was an example each day of drive and professionalism.

She was laser-focused on organizing our IT strategy, consolidating resources, being good stewards for the organization, and making real change. She was regularly the only woman in a room full of men, and I watched her get denied promotion opportunities time and time again while holding her head high, never complaining. She took it on the chin, leveled up, and moved forward each time.

She also always put me in positions where I could change and grow. I was her number two, and she was the Director of IT for the region. I sat in hospital boardrooms with her, met with hospital executives, reported on and strategized the IT plan for the hospital systems.

I can still smell the leather on the chairs, the clean, polished wooden executive desk in those formal boardrooms, and how grateful I felt every time I pulled up my chair next to Stephanie's. Here I was, a woman who had started as a medical assistant, now sitting at tables where million-dollar decisions were being made, contributing to strategic planning for major healthcare systems.

This was the role I was in during 2020 when the world shut down. Stephanie didn't blink. She expected and required us to suit up, mask up, come into the hospital, and provide all the IT support needed to care for patients. Even when I hesitated, she let the team know: "This is what we do. This is what we are called to do."

I even remember her saying we should only work from home for a couple of weeks, which still makes me laugh as I am now a full-time remote consultant five years later. But that remote opportunity was one of the catalysts for me taking the leap into the consulting space.

Taking the position as an analyst was my first bet on myself. Accepting leadership positions was my second bet. Leaving that health system for a new company and title was my third bet. And now, joining the world of consulting was going to be the biggest bet of my professional life.

Working under a leader like Stephanie — a wife, a mother, and the most dedicated leader I had witnessed to date —

inspired me to continue to bet on myself, to hold myself to no limits, and to understand that even if I have setbacks, even if there are often too many men at the table, I should hold my ground and keep moving forward no matter what.

I remember sitting with her once we were able to get back out in the world. She invited me to her country club for a late lunch and a drink to celebrate the time we had worked together and the relationship we had built. I even tried to talk her into joining the world of consulting. She appreciated it, but Stephanie at her core was and is so loyal, so dedicated to working and growing for an organization she believes in. She had climbed the ladder and supported her family through dedication and persistence.

My admiration and respect for Stephanie during the time I worked with her was exactly what I needed for the next trajectory of my life.

Watching Stephanie navigate her own professional battles while simultaneously lifting me was one of the most powerful leadership lessons I've ever received. She was overqualified for so many positions that went to less experienced men. She had the vision, the strategy, the track record, and the results, but time after time, I watched her get passed over for promotions that should have been hers.

But here's what made Stephanie extraordinary: she never let those setbacks diminish her investment in others. She never became bitter or stopped advocating for her team. She never pulled back from developing talent because she wasn't getting the recognition she deserved. Instead, she doubled down on excellence, on strategic thinking, on positioning herself and her team for success.

She taught me something profound about leadership: that lifting while you climb isn't conditional on your own advancement. You don't stop being a champion for others just because you're facing your own professional battles. You don't withhold mentorship just because the system isn't treating you fairly.

Stephanie taught me what it means to be a "woman's woman" in the truest sense. She used her position to create opportunities for me, to expose me to executive-level decision-making, to prepare me for leadership roles that I might not have imagined were possible. She did this while facing her own glass ceilings, her own frustrations, her own career obstacles.

The fact that she told me to "know my worth and how to negotiate" before I even started working for her speaks volumes about her character. She wanted me to succeed not just in the role, but in understanding my own value. She wanted me to step into that six-figure position with confidence, knowing that I had earned it and deserved it.

That's what extraordinary leaders do: they celebrate your growth even when it takes you away from them. They invest in your potential even when they're fighting their own battles. They model resilience and persistence even when the system isn't fair to them.

Stephanie taught me that betting on yourself isn't a one-time decision; it's a series of choices to keep growing, keep reaching, keep believing in your own potential even when external validation doesn't come as quickly as it should. She taught me that sometimes the most powerful thing you can do is hold your head high, keep delivering excellent work, and continue to lift others even when you're not getting the recognition you deserve.

Thank you, Stephanie, for mentoring me in negotiation before I even started the job. Thank you for giving me my first six-figure salary and for teaching me to know my worth. Thank you for putting me in positions to grow, for including me in executive-level strategy sessions, for treating me as your trusted second-in-command.

Thank you for showing me what it looks like to navigate professional setbacks with grace and dignity. Thank you for proving that being passed over for promotions doesn't mean you stop being excellent, stop developing others, or stop positioning yourself for future opportunities.

Thank you for using your position to lift others while climbing your own mountain, investing in potential even while facing your own obstacles, celebrating others' success even when your own recognition was delayed.

And thank you for inspiring me to take that biggest bet of my life — to leap into consulting, to believe in unlimited potential, to understand that sometimes you have to bet on yourself when the traditional path isn't moving fast enough.

Today, you are operating at the highest level of leadership at the same hospital system, and there is no one who deserves it more. Your persistence, your excellence, your unwavering commitment to developing others while navigating your own challenges all led to the recognition and advancement you had earned years before it was finally given to you.

You were extraordinary in the most ordinary way.. Your example of fighting your own battles while lifting me taught me much of what I needed to know about true leadership, resilience, and the power of investing in others even when your own path is challenging.

The foundation you built, the confidence you instilled, the strategic thinking you modeled, prepared me for the consulting world where I would need to bet on myself again and again. You didn't just give me a job and a salary; you gave me a masterclass in leadership, resilience, and the courage to keep reaching for more.

# CHAPTER
## *Nine*

## "Unlimited Potential"

It was 2020, and I was taking the chance to join the world of consulting. I signed up with a consulting firm and was assigned to a project manager position for a large ambulatory go-live. It was the largest the company had done to date. It was fully remote because of the pandemic, and I was anxious and nervous to prove myself. Although I was comfortable with local systems, I was unsure how my skills would translate into a new environment.

I hit the ground sprinting. This project really needed help. It was in a critical state, and I immediately took charge, implementing servant leadership right away, listening to the struggles of the analysts, and building friendships that I still have today. There was an executive consulting leader at my company who took notice right away: Kristen.

I was being assigned additional tasks and duties and was happy to jump in and help get the project across the finish line. In this space of consulting, you simply need to jump in and take charge. There is rarely someone going to give you affirmation or thanks. You need to be confident enough in your ability and keep moving forward, being a leader full of integrity.

In the midst of the go-live stress, I received a package. It was a thank you from Kristen: a tumbler, snacks, a candle, and other notes of gratitude. She simply noted: "We would not have crossed the finish line without you."

I had witnessed her leadership over the months I was working, and that tip of the hat to me, those simple words of acknowledgment, was yet another confirmation of the leader she was.

After that gig was completed, I was assigned to a couple of other projects, flexing my consulting muscle in other spaces with other health systems and leaders. A couple of projects later, I would find myself in a project that was nearing its end. I had given everything I had, but the leadership of the company we were serving wasn't ready for the change required to have a successful go-live.

I was looking through some documents and I noticed a familiar name: Kristen. It was a project that was done months before. I gave her a call. We had stayed in touch via text here and there, but now I needed her advice.

"Kristen, how are you?! Were you working on this project on the east coast? I saw your name!"

She said she had been, but when she got the opportunity to work with a new consulting company in a leadership role, she was tackling a large new project out in California. Then she mentioned that they needed someone to step in and help manage the tech space.

It was serendipity. I was in.

I joined her at another very large, complicated go-live, and we were back in the trenches together. This time I worked with her more closely. As she got to know me and my skills better, and I got to know hers, she promoted and positioned me to start networking with other women leaders. She was planting seeds, nudging me that I needed to be in strategic and advisory roles. She, as many leaders before her, saw yet another level of potential in me that I had not yet seen.

I had worked with many male leaders and consultants, all of whom thought highly of me, but none of whom took the time she did to say, "Hey, what's your plan here? You need to be thinking bigger."

During that time, I noticed something about Kristen that I admire immensely. Kristen is an executive-level advisor in rooms where critical conversations are had and strategic decisions are made, driving change for healthcare safety and billion-dollar outcomes. Yet when a small clinic was suffering at go-live and our firm was expected to provide top support, she drove there, met with physicians, and gave support however she could.

Kristen quietly and humbly is the driving force for change at all levels. Like Stephanie before her, she's often the only woman in the room. Still, she is  the sharpest, the most knowledgeable, and the driving force for change. Even when others at times get the spotlight, she would rather just keep moving, keep driving for higher levels of change and impact. The accolades are something she doesn't speak about, even though she has the right to.

After that engagement, there was another opportunity to work with her on another big organization healthcare project — different from a software go-live — and it revealed another level of my skillset. I once again watched her see the big picture and have tough conversations at all levels of the organization.

I said to her, "Kristen, I want you to know that I see you. None of this happens without you. You are a force, a boss, and an incredible woman who has created so much opportunity and potential for people around you, and you do it quietly and humbly."

At the time of this writing, I am working with her as a founding member of her tech startup company where she is the CEO. I had been working with her for months when she casually mentioned that she had been mentoring a couple of young consultants on the side who got unfair deals and wanted to assist in guiding them to their best next steps.

She was working full-time, running a company, being a wife, a mom, colleague, friend, sister, daughter, and didn't hesitate to lend her ear and time to young consultants in need of help, all while never boasting, bragging, or pushing herself for any recognition.

I see her for the amazing leader she is. Nothing gets by her. She operates with integrity, fairness, firmness, and with the most class I have ever witnessed.

I will continue to rock with Kristen for the rest of my personal and professional life, growing a brand together, growing a company together, supporting her. As wives and mothers of daughters, we understand each other. The doors Kristen has opened for me, the faith she has shown in my ability, the tables where she's arranged for me to sit, and the times she has put me at the helm, has inspired me in ways she will never understand.

And for that, I take it seriously to show good in response to the faith and trust she puts in me.

She would say she's ordinary, but extraordinary doesn't fully describe her. Kristen is one-of-one. I am deeply grateful that the universe has put us together in this lifetime.

Working with Kristen has taught me something profound about leadership at the highest levels. I've watched her navigate male-driven, C-suite environments with a combination of strategic brilliance and quiet confidence that commands respect without demanding attention. She doesn't need to be the loudest voice in the room because she's consistently the most prepared, the most insightful, the most solution-oriented.

What sets Kristen apart is her ability to see unlimited potential in others and then create the opportunities for that potential to flourish. When she told me I needed to think bigger, she didn't just plant the seed; she watered it with introductions to other strong women mentors in the industry, with strategic project assignments that stretched my capabilities, with constant encouragement to reach for roles I might not have imagined for myself.

The fact that she drove to that struggling clinic during a critical go-live, despite being an executive-level advisor responsible for billion-dollar outcomes, tells you everything you need to know about her leadership philosophy. She understands that real leadership happens at every level, that showing up for the people in the trenches is just as important as strategizing in the boardroom.

Her quiet mentorship of young consultants who got unfair deals, doing this on her own time while running a company and managing all her other responsibilities, is pure Kristen. She lifts while she climbs not because it's expected or because she gets recognition for it, but because that's who she is at her core.

As her Global Head of Branding and Partnerships at the startup, I get to witness her CEO leadership up close. She's building something innovative in healthcare technology while creating a culture where people can reach their unlimited potential. She's proving that women can drive billion-dollar outcomes and still be present personally for their teams, still take time to mentor others, still operate with the kind of integrity and class that inspires everyone around them.

The serendipity of that day when I saw her name on the project documents feels like more than coincidence now. It feels like the universe aligning to put me in the path of someone who would not just recognize my potential but actively create space for it to grow beyond what I thought possible.

Thank you, Kristen, for immediately recognizing my excellence when I was nervous about proving myself in consulting. Thank you for that package with the tumbler and candle and the note that said we wouldn't have crossed the finish line without me. You saw me and my contributions when I was still wondering if my skills would translate.

Thank you for planting seeds about thinking bigger, for introducing me to other strong women leaders, for positioning me in strategic and advisory roles when I was still seeing myself as just a project manager.

Thank you for driving to struggling clinics and meeting with physicians while also advising on billion-dollar decisions. You've shown me that real leadership means showing up at every level, that you never get too senior to care about the people in the trenches.

Thank you for quietly mentoring young consultants who need guidance, for operating with such integrity and class, for being the sharpest person in rooms full of men while never making it about recognition or ego.

And thank you for bringing me in as a founding member of your startup, for trusting me with the role of Global Head of Branding and Partnerships, for seeing unlimited potential in me and creating the platform where that potential can flourish.

You are extraordinary in the most ordinary way — simply being yourself, operating with integrity, lifting others while building something incredible, never seeking the spotlight while consistently being the driving force for change.

The combination of strategic brilliance, operational excellence, personal humility, and genuine investment in others' success is rare at any level, but especially rare at the executive level where you operate.

I am grateful every day that the universe put us together in this lifetime. Working alongside you, learning from you, building something meaningful together is the culmination of every lesson I learned from every extraordinary ordinary woman who came before.

You didn't just see my potential; you created unlimited space for it to grow. And for that, I will spend the rest of my career making good on the faith and trust you've placed in me.

# PART 4
## Heart and Home Foundation

# CHAPTER
## Ten

### "The Woman Who Brought Me
### Back to Life"

She was standing over him with a large cast iron skillet raised high over the head of her sleeping husband. As his chest rose and fell, she flashed back to the severe abuse that had started the night of her wedding as a teenage bride, arranged to marry the church deacon who was supposed to take care of her.

She pictured every time he struck her face and put his hands around her neck, every night of abuse that he inflicted on her and her children. She was going to end it. She was going to kill him and end the suffering for all of them.

As she raised the skillet up high, something held her back, the thought of her kids without a mom, afraid he would wake up and grab her, the punishment that would continue. With shaking hands, she dropped the frying pan and called her pastor.

He told her what any patriarchal Christian pastor told women in the 1960s: to stick it out, to stay, that this was her husband, to listen to him. She could not endure this anymore, and although the church turned its back on her, she would tell me later it was the people who betrayed her, not God.

"I don't understand why I did this," she told me years later, "but I ironed his work clothes the day I left. Then I packed my kids and myself and we left. I ironed his clothes, and then I left."

That was my grandmother, Freida.

In those times, to be a single woman with three kids was financially and socially devastating. The church rejected her, and yet she moved forward, ironing clothes for money and doing any job available to help support the kids. Although she left her abuser, the trauma would be carried in the hearts and minds of her and her three children for their lifetimes.

Her firstborn daughter, Pam, my mother, would also get married at a young age seventeen years old, and would suffer the loss of her first child, a baby girl in the late 1970s from SIDS.

When I was born several years later, I had breathing problems too, and my mom's PTSD paralyzed her from properly caring and assisting in all of my care. My grandma stepped in to help. When I did, in fact, quit breathing, it was my grandma who quite literally breathed life into my little body. Pinched my little nose, opened my mouth, inhaled and exhaled life into my lungs.

She nurtured me, and from the beginning, we shared a maternal bond stronger than earthly explanation. Her breathing physical life into me would be the perfect metaphor that started our connection throughout my life.

My dad was in and out of our lives. My parents married and divorced twice before I had a single memory, and so Grandmother stepped in to help raise me every step of the way. We always lived close to my grandmother and sometimes lived with her. She cooked for me, picked me up from school, loved me and was there for me all along the way.

Despite what she had been through, my grandmother was a woman of faith. Her prayers, I'm convinced, kept me safe throughout my lifetime. I never heard her raise her voice, never once heard her yell at a single soul in my entire lifetime. I only ever saw her cry twice: once when my aunt, her baby girl, flew out of state to live for a while, and once when I sat by her side in 2015 when she was diagnosed with cancer with less than 30 days left on this earth.

I held her during that time, remembering all of the years she had poured into me and all the phone calls I made to her. I cried to her hysterically when life had completely broken me. She stood by me as a teenager when I was making bad decisions, always unequivocally just showed up for me, listened, encouraged, prayed, and never judged me.

She believed in me in a way that was unshakeable and fierce. She spoke life into me in my darkest days when I wanted to give up. She was always proud. She remained full of love and faith that I was an extraordinary person with an extraordinary life ahead of me, especially when I wasn't sure of my own self-worth.

We were a poor family from humble means, and I always wanted to make her proud.

I remember when I purchased my first home. It was a 2,800 square foot, two-story, brick front home with five bedrooms, four full bathrooms, and two fireplaces in a beautiful suburban area. A modest home by some standards, but to my grandma it was more than she could imagine.

I'll never forget when she pulled into my driveway for the first time and I went out to greet her. The look on her face was so full of pride, love, and joy. We didn't have it fully furnished yet, and I can still picture her sitting in my living room on a wooden kitchen chair, knitting a blanket. I was in the kitchen just watching her, so content, taking it all in.

I would not understand until later, when I was a parent, what that moment really meant to her. It meant that all the years she poured into me, all the years she loved me and spoke life into me, worried about me and shed silent tears alone in the night over me were not wasted. When I was a young adult making mistakes, having a baby while I was so young, she remained an unwavering rock of love, the example of a true believer.

She always fed anyone who was hungry, taking care of all the kids in the neighborhood, loving on all those around her. She never met a stranger and truly loved all she came in contact with. And they all loved her. But there was something special about the way she loved me. As a medium would later tell me, we were twin flames in this lifetime.

So it was only right that she could count on me to support her through her end of life.

I remember the last ride home, just her and I, from the hospital when we found out "there is nothing more to be done." It was nighttime on a long country road when my heart spilled over.

I said, "I love you, Gram."

She paused for a minute and said, "There's not enough love in this world to go around to explain what I feel for you."

What she didn't know is that I was recording our conversation. Her last words to me would be forever preserved. When I think about her, how grateful I am that I had someone who loved me unconditionally. Truly unconditionally. It would be the template for how I approached love for the people in my life.

My grandma didn't have money, a poor woman with humble means and a humble beginning but her impact on my life was far greater than money can buy. I kept that close to my heart, knowing that no matter how much material possessions I gain, nothing is more important than unconditional love, honor, and respect for all that my grandmother was.

She was a lover, a gardener, a cook, a nurse, a counselor, mother, sister, friend, neighbor, safe haven, selfless, giving with every ounce of her life. Her sacrifice is always at the forefront of my mind. When I am heading to work, flying first class, talking to a group of women, interacting with those less fortunate, I always silently say: "Grandma, you would be so proud. I am living out beyond your wildest dreams for what I could achieve. All the sacrifices you made were not in vain. I carry you with me throughout my life and will honor your life and love in everything that I do."

Looking back now at my journey through all the extraordinary ordinary women who lifted me, I understand that none of it would have been possible without Frieda's foundation. Robin could recognize leadership in me because Frieda had already told me I was extraordinary. Donna could give me hard truths because Frieda had taught me that love sometimes looks like difficult conversations. Kathy could keep the door open for my future because Frieda had always kept her heart open for who I could become.

Every woman who invested in me, believed in me, lifted me while they climbed . They were all building on the bedrock of unconditional love that Frieda established. She helped me understand what it meant to be loved without condition, without judgment, without reservation. That foundation made me capable of receiving love, recognizing it, appreciating it, and eventually giving it.

The trauma that Freida endured in the arranged marriage, the abuse, the abandonment by her church when she chose freedom over suffering could have made her bitter, closed, afraid to love deeply. Instead, it made her treasure love more fiercely, pour it out more generously, fight for it more courageously.

When she breathed life into my infant body, she was doing more than performing CPR. She was breathing into me her own capacity for resilience, her own belief in possibility, her own understanding that love is stronger than trauma, that hope is more powerful than fear, that one person's unwavering faith in another can literally change the trajectory of a life.

Every phone call when I was crying and broken, every moment she stood by me through bad decisions, every time she spoke life into me when I couldn't see my own worth. She was teaching me how to receive love, how to trust it, how to believe I was worthy of it. Without that foundation, I never would have been able to accept the mentorship, guidance, and investment that all those professional women offered me.

Freida didn't live to see me become Global Head of Branding and Partnerships at a startup, didn't see me speaking to groups of women leaders, didn't see me flying first class to consulting engagements. But she saw something more important: she saw the woman I was becoming. She saw the potential that all those other women would eventually recognize and nurture.

Her last words to me — "There's not enough love in this world to go around to explain what I feel for you" — weren't just about the depth of her love. They were about the limitlessness of it, the way it transcended any boundary, any condition, any circumstance. That kind of love becomes the foundation for everything else.

When Cecelia promoted me swiftly through the analyst ranks, when Ellen walked beside me through college and career growth, when Stephanie positioned me for executive-level opportunities, when Kristen saw unlimited potential, they were all able to invest in me because Frieda had already invested everything she had.

She taught me that extraordinary doesn't mean famous or wealthy or publicly recognized. Extraordinary means loving without limit, giving without reservation, believing without proof. Extraordinary means breathing life into others, literally and metaphorically, again and again and again.

109

My grandmother was extraordinary in the most ordinary way. She was simply a woman who chose love over bitterness, hope over despair, giving over taking. She was a woman who understood that sometimes the most powerful thing you can do is believe in someone's future when their present is broken, love them through their mistakes, and never, ever give up on who they can become.

Thank you, Freida, for breathing life into me that first time when my infant lungs failed. Thank you for continuing to breathe life into me every time I lost my way, lost my hope, lost my faith in myself.

Thank you for creating the foundation that made every other relationship in this book possible. Every woman who lifted me was building on the bedrock you laid, adding to the structure you began, contributing to the person you always knew I could become.

Thank you for understanding that my success was never just about me. It was about honoring your sacrifice, proving your faith, making your love worthwhile.

I carry you with me in everything I do, Grandma. When I lift others, I'm using hands you taught to give. When I believe in someone's potential, I'm using eyes you taught to see. When

I love without condition, I'm using a heart you filled to overflowing.

You were the first extraordinary ordinary woman in my life, and you made all the others possible. Your granddaughter is thriving because of your sacrifices, succeeding because of your love, leading because you first led her to believe in herself.

All the sacrifices you made were not in vain. I carry you with me always, and I will honor your life and love in everything that I do.

# CHAPTER
## Eleven

"The Resilience I Didn't Understand"

December 22, 2003. I held a little human life in my arms that I had been cultivating inside my body for nine months and two days. My immediate thought was to apologize to my mom for every time I was late, every time I told her I hated her in teenage angst, for holding her accountable for all the wrongs in my childhood.

I had no idea until that moment the way she loved, how the culmination of her life had set her up to endure so much suffering while trying to parent and love me. It was a moment where I understood my mom and her sacrifices for the first time.

My mother, Pamela, was fifteen years old when a cop woke her up on a park bench in San Francisco, California. She and a friend had hitchhiked there from northern Michigan. She was running away from the deep pain of a traumatic childhood and abuse at the hands of her father and the men in her life. Each mile she traveled, she was trying to forget about the pain, the way she felt disregarded and dismissed.

Her first and only airplane ride would be as a teenager in handcuffs, being flown home back to the place of her pain.

There had to be another way. When she met Dan at sixteen years old, he was the answer  a carefree, gregarious man who was fun, exciting, and an escape. She married him with her mom's permission, repeating the generational pattern of her time, and became a teenage bride as her mother before her.

Before the age of twenty-one, she would give birth to a baby boy. Later, she had a baby girl who died of SIDS one month after childbirth. Before she could take a legal drink herself, she was married to an alcoholic with one baby boy and one dead child.

I had no idea when I was a simple light being born in September of 1981 that the woman holding me had experienced insurmountable trauma, that she had suffered a lifetime of pain before the moment we met.

She and my dad would divorce before I could remember, and my childhood was errant, moving from place to place. Apartment to apartment. My mother, carrying the baggage of generations before her, would work hard to provide. It took everything she could to make the rent and pay for electricity and gas. Since counseling, self-love, and worth were not topics for women in the 1980s, she swallowed her trauma, leaving no room for emotional availability to support and comfort her young daughter.

My own emotions and inability to articulate the pain of my life would be taken out on her regularly. She didn't understand me, she didn't know how to comfort me, she was the scapegoat to blame for my lot in life, for being poor, for it all.

That is, until... until I too became a young mother. Until I saw my mom as a woman, not the person who was responsible for my success and failures. That was up to me. Finally, I would see her as the woman she truly was. A woman who sacrificed her entire life to work and provide. A woman who stood by me, her daughter, at every teacher conference, every school event, every cheerleading competition, every late night she spent worrying, every mistake, every victory, and every time, she was there.

I stopped seeing what she didn't provide and realized that what she was able to do was a miracle. The pain from her past, the pain of losing a child, of abuse, of living through my brother's abuse, she was a survivor. She is one of the strongest women to walk the earth, a blue-collar, gritty, hard-working, sacrificing survivor who is the most extraordinary ordinary woman I know.

Like her mother, she gave and loved selflessly to those in need, even when she didn't have much herself. She still does.

Walking around her small town with her now, she still shows me off with pride: "This is my daughter, Mandy." Each person we meet tells me where they know her, how they worked with her, and how much they love her.

The revelation that came with holding my own daughter was this: my mother had been doing the impossible all along. She had been loving me through her own unhealed trauma, providing for me while carrying the weight of generational pain, showing up for me while battling her own demons.

As a fifteen-year-old on that park bench in San Francisco, she had been a child herself, running from abuse that no child should ever endure. As a teenage bride, she was repeating patterns she had no tools to break. As a young

116

mother losing her baby girl to SIDS, she was experiencing a grief that would have broken many people completely.

And yet, when I came along, she found the strength to be present. Not perfect. She couldn't give me the emotional availability I craved because she was still learning how to survive her own emotional wounds. But she gave me what she could: consistency, provision, presence at every important moment.

I spent my childhood and teenage years angry at her for what felt like emotional distance, for what seemed like her inability to understand my pain. What I couldn't see then was that she was drowning in her own pain while still managing to keep me afloat.

Every teacher conference she attended while working multiple jobs. Every cheerleading competition she made it to despite her exhaustion. Every time she came through when life knocked me down, even when I blamed her for my struggles. Every sacrifice she made to ensure we had a roof over our heads and food on the table, even when it meant she went without.

She was extraordinary in the most ordinary way, simply refusing to give up. On herself, on her children, on the possibility that life could be better than the trauma she had inherited.

The moment I became a mother, I understood that her love had always been there, steady and unwavering, even when it didn't look like what I thought I needed. Her love was in the showing up, the providing, the never giving up, even when everything in her past told her that love leads to pain and abandonment leads to safety.

She broke generational cycles simply by staying. By working. By being present at my events. By never abandoning me, even when I was at my worst. By loving me through her own unhealed wounds and figuring out how to be a mother while still healing from being a traumatized child herself.

Today, I see a blue-collar warrior who fought battles I never knew about while still making sure I knew she was proud of me.

I see a woman who, despite every reason to become bitter, closed, and self-protective, chose to remain open to love. Who chose to invest in her children's futures even when her own past was full of pain.

Thank you, Mom, for being a survivor. Thank you for fighting, for not giving up on yourself, and in turn, not giving up on me. Thank you for showing up at every event, for working multiple jobs to provide, for being proud of me even when I couldn't see past my own pain to appreciate yours.

Thank you for breaking cycles you didn't even know you were breaking, for choosing love over bitterness, for choosing presence over abandonment, for choosing to invest in my future even when your past was full of trauma.

Thank you for being extraordinary in the most ordinary way simply by never giving up, by loving imperfectly but consistently, by proving that resilience can be passed down just as surely as trauma can.

You were the foundation beneath the foundation, the strength that taught me how to recognize strength in others, the love that prepared me to receive love from all the women who would lift me throughout my career.

Your resilience became my resilience. Your refusal to give up became my determination to keep going. Your love, imperfect but unwavering, became the template that helped me recognize and appreciate every extraordinary ordinary woman who would invest in my potential.

You are one of the strongest women to walk this earth, and I am proud to be your daughter. Salute.

# CHAPTER
## *Twelve*

## "The Light Switch"

Mariona was nineteen years old, 1.5 years into college, when she knew it wasn't for her. She had followed this path because she knew that's what her parents wanted, what they expected, what her whole family was looking for her to do. She made the phone call to me, her mother, saying that she could not go on this path anymore. She was dropping out of school and going to get her esthetician's license, go into the workforce, and begin life on her own.

I supported her and encouraged her on the outside, but inside I was broken. What was it all for? What did I do all of this for?

She moved back home while finishing vocational school, and one evening we had a deep conversation.

"Mom, I know this isn't the path you and dad wanted for me, but it was never the path I wanted for myself. I always just fell in line with what you wanted me to do, attend the schools you wanted me to attend despite me not feeling like I belonged. I did the activities you expected me to do and made the post-high school choices everyone was expecting me to make. I feel like you did everything you thought was right for me but didn't always see ME."

I wanted to get defensive, to tell her that I did everything I could with the best of intentions and I sacrificed so much so she could make good choices. But instead, I listened. And I cried. And I asked her to forgive me.

Why? Because she was right. I knew in that moment what she needed from me was to simply be seen. She needed me to acknowledge her and let her know: I see you, I support you, and if I could change it I would, but moving forward I can be here for you unconditionally, and I always will.

Mariona has been out on her own now for a while. As a mature mom now, looking back at the young mom I was, I wish I could tell her to let go, it's going to be alright. I wish I knew to listen to her, meet her where she is, and watch her become her own individual wonderful self because that is what she and everyone truly deserves. I really did have the best of intentions.

But let me go back to the beginning, to understand how we got to that conversation.

December 22, 2003. I can still see her big brown eyes looking up at me the moment I held her skin to skin. From her very first breath, her eyes were wide and full of life, as if she already understood the world she was entering. In that moment, I knew what sacrificial love felt like. I knew I would give my life and take a life to defend her. I knew I had never experienced such an overwhelming need to protect. I was in love, and I was scared.

After her physical exam, they wheeled her back into the room to me, wrapped tightly in a pink blanket with a large pink pacifier covering most of her sweet face. Wow! An entire little human, outside of my body, my responsibility to love and protect.

Like the generations of women before me, as a young mother twenty-two years of age, carrying my own unidentified trauma, I decided to pour my entire efforts in life to ensure she would not experience the kind of life I did. Every wrong I felt I had suffered in my childhood, I would somehow make right. Up until the time of her birth, I had no real direction in my life. I didn't feel worthy myself to have vision. But as soon as Mariona became part of the equation, she became the reason, my drive to ensure she had a family to support her, a mom and dad who were present, a safe home, never lacking or feeling othered.

I was trying to heal my past, and, in that, I was not yet able to see or understand that my needs, what I lacked, are not the same as hers. She's a separate and individual being and would have her own needs. I worked so hard to climb ladders, get multiple degrees, to be an example, a mother she could be proud of, with the expectation she would fit into my expectations of who I thought she should be because of my decisions and sacrifices.

What I learned is that, as a woman, you should never make decisions or put your expectations of sacrifice on your child. They cannot fix your broken heart and right the wrongs. She was an individual who fought her own battles, and even though she had it "way better" than I did, that didn't mean she wouldn't feel pain and struggle and make different decisions than the ones I had drawn out in my head and heart.

Loving her meant loving her where she is, not where I placed her. The unconditional love my grandmother offered me was the kind of love she actually needed. Her mistakes didn't mean I was a failure. Showing up and giving her space to grow was all she ever needed.

Now, as an emerging adult, Mari is forging her own path. I have grown to understand that she is my teacher in this lifetime. She has taught me how to become a mentor, a cheerleader, and encourager. I was a young mother not knowing how to mother. I made my mistakes, but I am hoping that one day she will look back as I did with my mom and realize the same thing I have: that a mother is just a woman, a human being, a flawed life force trying to pour everything they know into protecting and loving the only way they know how.

Mari, thank you for loving me. Thank you for teaching me to give you space, to simply be there to support and not judge, to understand that unsolicited advice can feel like criticism, and to trust that I will be present when you ask for it.

Thank you for being the greatest joy I have ever experienced. Watching you grow, laugh, cry, and push forward through your hardest times has been my reminder never to give up on myself. You are the reason I know that life holds so much more.

You are your own woman with your own dreams, and until my very last breath, I will be here, right by your side, because, baby girl, there is not enough love in this world to explain how I feel for you.

The moment you were placed in my arms was like a light switch being flipped in my soul. Everything I had worked toward, every struggle I had endured, every mistake I had made suddenly had purpose. You didn't just change my priorities; you gave me priorities for the very first time in my life.

Before her, I was drifting, reacting, surviving. After her, I was purposeful, intentional, driven. Every career move, every educational goal, every decision was filtered through one question: "What kind of example am I setting for her?"

But in my fierce determination to give her everything I didn't have, I initially missed something crucial: she wasn't me. She didn't need me to fix my childhood through hers. She needed me to see her, support her, and love her for exactly who she was becoming.

The hardest lesson of motherhood was learning to separate my healing from her happiness, my dreams from her destiny, my fears from her freedom. I had to learn that loving her unconditionally meant accepting that she might make choices I wouldn't make, follow paths I hadn't planned, become someone different from what I had envisioned.

Watching her grow into her own person has been both my greatest joy and my most humbling experience. Every time I tried to direct her story, she taught me to trust her story. Every time I projected my fears onto her future, she taught me her own courage. Every time I wanted to fix her struggles, she demonstrated her own resilience.

She became my teacher in the most unexpected way not by being the perfect daughter, but by being the authentic person she was designed to be. She taught me that motherhood isn't about creating a mini-me or healing my wounds through someone else's life. It's about witnessing another soul's journey and offering support without trying to control the destination.

The moment I held her, I thought my job was to protect her from everything I had experienced. What I learned is that my job was to love her through everything she would experience which would be her own unique combination of joys and struggles, victories and challenges, completely separate from mine.

Mari, you saved me from giving up on myself by giving me someone more important than myself to live for. But more than that, you taught me how to live—not just survive, not just react, not just cope, but truly live with purpose, intention, and love.

You were extraordinary in the most ordinary way simply by being yourself, by growing into who you were meant to be, by teaching me that the greatest gift we can give someone is the freedom to be authentically themselves.

Thank you for being my light switch, my teacher, my greatest joy, and my constant reminder that love isn't about control or expectations; it's about presence, support, and the courage to let someone become who they're meant to be.

I will repeat, because I can't say it enough, "There's not enough love in this world to go around to explain how I feel for you" — Freida's words to me, now mine to you, the continuation of unconditional love passed down through generations of extraordinary ordinary women.

# CHAPTER
## *Thirteen*

## "Three Decades of Sisterhood"

It was the 1996-1997 school year and I was in the tenth grade. The year I transferred to Wyoming Park. The year I needed a fresh start. Right away at Wyoming Park High School, I met a couple of people I thought were "cool," and we got along right away. One of them, Colleen, called Coco, introduced me during gym class to a very quiet, very sweet girl.

She said, "This is Marie. She is an angel, literally."

I looked at Marie. I can still see her beautiful face and bright smile. I truly liked her immediately.

*Mandy Crosby*

At fifteen years old, Marie was, by all accounts, an angel and the opposite of what I was at that moment. Marie was an excellent student. She took advanced classes, came from a two-parent household, and lived in a nice home in a beautiful suburban neighborhood. In almost all ways, she was a juxtaposition of me.

By this age, I had lived in over a dozen apartments, homes, and family houses. I had drank, smoked weed, and was barely getting by, narrowly passing my classes. For all the differences between us, there were so many foundational things that brought us together. We had the same sense of humor, we laughed at the same lines in a movie, at the awkwardness of various situations. From the beginning, we couldn't explain it, but we saw each other as each other stood. We respected, appreciated, and laughed together. Our bond began.

She once told me that I was the first white girl she met who understood what she meant when she said, "perming her hair." I grew up very close to a Black family when I was in elementary school and junior high, and my knowledge and respect of Marie's culture bonded us deeper as she was often the only representation in the majority of spaces, classes, and experiences growing up in a predominantly white area.

We still discuss how she and I would go out to eat, shopping, and generally hang out together in high school, and people would stop and stare. We would joke that they must have never seen best friends of different races together before. We didn't discuss much deeper than that at the time. We were focused on what most teenage girls were: music, going to the mall, testing our freedom, and of course, boys.

From tenth grade year up until the day Marie left for college, we were inseparable. I was at her house as much as she was at mine, going out to eat with each other's families, going on family trips, going out to teen clubs of the day, dancing, staying out too late, getting in trouble, being fully embedded in each other's lives and families, and having the time of our lives.

I can still feel how my heart broke when she left for school. I would, of course, visit her in college, attend some parties, and as we would affectionately call it, "pulling books" when we would do something crazy or memorable that we would never speak of again.

I was always in awe of her, and envious in many ways, shopping with her for her dorm room, helping her move from place to place as she took one step after another toward her college degree. Our lives were in contrast: I went to vocational school and made some crazy choices that led to me being a young mom trying to make it day by day.

But no matter how different life's course would lead us, the foundation we built our friendship on remained. We were never jealous of each other, never felt anger, envy, or hate. All we knew was that one of our successes or victories felt like the other's success and wins. That's why I cheered the loudest in the room at MSU the day she walked across the stage. That's why she was one of the few who celebrated at my baby shower, held and loved my daughter right away, while she launched her own journey in life.

As I was starting a family and getting by, Marie would again make a decision to branch out in life, She announced she was moving to Georgia. Once again, I was going to miss her so much. During these years, we did the best we could to stay in touch, but we were both on our journeys of finding ourselves and surviving.

What we didn't know or talk about as teenagers was that we both actually carried trauma that would show itself in how we were learning to live life as adults. As Marie would have her first son, she would come home for a bit, and I would be there by her side changing her baby's first diaper. She would then make a move back to Georgia and would eventually have a second baby boy.

We were both in various stages of survival mode, and the physical distance had become daily distance. We talked less frequently. I would not find out until later that Marie was fighting and overcoming battles I could not imagine. She was the protector of her two sons and would escape a situation that could have taken her life and changed the course of the lives of her children.

I remember the phone call when she told me everything about what she had survived, what she was going through, and how she felt alone. I was overcome with grief, feeling desperate to try and make this better for her, to go back and be present for her, to want so badly to have protected her. But striving to change the past is futile. I was in my own struggle at the time, trying to provide for my daughter, putting my family on my back to provide. I went back to school full time, which left no capacity for me or her at the time to be fully present. We had lost keeping regularly in touch but never lost love.

We would check in with each other over the years, but it was 2020 that would bring us back to each other. God's plan. That was the year that challenged us but ultimately strengthened our bonds with the people who mean the most, the very foundation of our lives: those who cheered us on; those who had always wanted us to win; those who desired the same things: love, equality, and peace in our families' lives and the lives of our children.

When we connected that year, we needed each other the same way we did when we were kids. Our children were older, and we were navigating life very differently as women in our thirties, both striving for growth and change in this act two of life.

We would have deep conversations about how our lives had been. We were open and honest with each other about the pains we had experienced. We cried together hard. We grieved lives that would have been. We grew together and have supported each other in the ways we did in youth, with a much wiser lens.

Now, each and every day, we walk beside each other, seeing each other through parenting our aging parents, seeing kids off to college, grieving, accomplishing personal and professional goals. There is no conversation, no topic, that we cannot bring to each other. We hold each other accountable, cheer each other on with the selfless giving of true unconditional love.

This friendship that has spanned three decades has been the foundation that I always come back to. Marie has seen me at every phase of life: the teenager that was wild and unsure, the young woman making questionable decisions, the determined mother, the career woman. She told me once, "You are not the same person. You have grown and changed in the most extraordinary way."

Her seeing me in that moment, her recognizing where I have been, the decisions I have made both bad, good, and indifferent, meant a lot. She had seen it all and been with me since "day one." "Day one" is not just a saying for us. She really has been right by my side, in my heart and my mind, through it all.

We are both now accomplished women in our forties with corporate careers, master's degrees, and amazing kids to be proud of. But we can still see each other in that gym that day. It's still 1997. We see all the pain, all the joy, all the growth, all the youth, all the love, all the laughter, all the grief and joy that the ride of life serves.

This has been God's divine plan all along, having her by my side, the one that is always on my team, the one that sees me exactly who I am, where I've been and where I am going, and loves me just where I am, always. There is no greater sisterhood in this life.

Marie inspires me. She motivates me. Her story, her beauty inside and out, is the very definition of one that deserves to be told and celebrated. No matter where we are in space and time, she has always had my back, and she remains my forever best friend, the one who reminds me to "dance".

What Marie represents in my life goes beyond friendship. She represents the power of seeing and being seen, of loving and being loved through every season, every mistake, every triumph, every transformation.

In a world where relationships often fade with distance, time, or changing circumstances, Marie and I have proven that true sisterhood transcends all of that. We've loved each other through different life stages, different choices, different struggles, and different successes.

She has been my constant—the person who knew me when I was wild and searching, who cheered for me when I found my direction, who held space for me when I was struggling, and who celebrates with me now as we've both become the women we always had the potential to be.

The beauty of our friendship is that it has never been competitive. Her success has always felt like my success. Her pain has always been my pain. Her joy has always been my joy. That kind of love is rare and precious.

Through three decades, Marie has been extraordinary in the most ordinary way — simply by being present, by loving without judgment, by seeing me through every phase and loving me exactly where I was in each one.

She has shown me what it means to have a sister by choice, a friend who becomes family, a person who holds your history and still believes in your future. She has been my mirror, reflecting back to me my growth, my strength, and my worth when I couldn't see it myself.

Thank you, Marie, for almost thirty years of unconditional friendship. Thank you for seeing me in that gym in 1997 and choosing to love me through every version of myself that followed. Thank you for being my constant, my cheerleader, my sister by choice.

Thank you for surviving your own battles and coming back to me, for being brave enough to share your pain and for trusting me to hold it with you. Thank you for growing with me, for changing with me, and for loving me through every season.

You have been extraordinary in the most ordinary way — simply by being yourself, by staying true to our friendship, by choosing love over judgment, presence over distance, and sisterhood over everything else.

There is no greater sisterhood in this life, and I am grateful every day that God's divine plan included you by my side. "Day one" isn't just a saying for us  it's a promise, a commitment, a love that has lasted three decades and will last the rest of our lives.

"I hope you dance," best friend. Always and forever.

# CHAPTER
## *Fourteen*

## "Sister of My Heart"

Approximately four years after my husband and I met, moved to Ohio and back, had a daughter, and overcame our own personal struggles, his youngest brother started dating a woman named Valencia. Their story wasn't that different from ours in that they met and would quickly commit and get pregnant.

When Valencia and I first met, we were both young women with our own respective traumas and life obstacles. I was twenty-four to twenty-five years old, and she was just nineteen. Looking back, we both approached the relationship with preconceived ideas and didn't quite understand each other's rhythm.

The beginning of the relationship would cause tension between my husband and his brother, as well as between her and me. At one point, as young families transitioning from place to place, we all ended up under the same roof at my in-laws—us with our toddler girl and them with their new baby girl. It all felt like a little too much as we navigated early parenthood, trying to find our way in the world without feeling "less than" or in competition with the other.

There was constant miscommunication and tension on both sides as each family would try to do the right thing. We attended each other's birthday parties and had weddings just weeks apart in 2010. Even during those celebrations, we all attended as family is obligated to do, but none of our hearts had yet been able to see the others' true intentions. We were all still too busy jockeying for a position in life, in the family, in society's eyes positions that we would come to realize never really mattered.

Valencia gave birth to two more kids: a boy and another baby girl. As kids often do, the kids' activities frequently brought us together at family events, holidays, and birthdays. As Valencia was growing in her career, she decided to become a medical assistant, and she and I worked together after I referred her to the office.

Despite our feelings of perceived differences, I wanted to see her win. I loved my nieces and nephew. We interacted with each other daily, learning each other in a new way. Life was teaching us lessons about what it really meant to be family, how our young selves, full of ego, couldn't see that each of us had such a love for helping others. We had both had difficult upbringings and traumas we were trying to overcome. In a world that was set against us failing, we were starting to realize we were the support and camaraderie needed to get through this life together. It was important that our kids loved each other and supported each other. That started us down the road toward being united, having a sisterly bond, with our hearts being open and softened to seeing the other person for who they truly were.

I never would have guessed the way I would need her in my life, how time and time again she has shown up  sometimes being the only one, not only for me but for my daughter. She has been a support system in areas of life that I, as a mother, have not.

We have become a safe space for each other, navigating marriage, in-laws, kids growing up, graduating high school, moving to college, and all the silent battles we face sometimes as women. We have and always will be there for each other through it all.

Today, there is an unspoken sense of connection between the two of us. There's no questioning our loyalty or our love for each other. We have seen friends and even family come and go, but there is a steadfastness in our bond that cannot be broken.

She has watched my journey of growth from young, struggling mom trying to find my way to pushing the limits in life, finding doors to open and kick down for her kids and mine. Her kids are like my own, and I find inspiration in loving them and being the best aunt I can be, as she is for my daughter.

There isn't a holiday, birthday, milestone, sporting event, or life event that goes by when we are not supporting each other in some capacity. Knowing I can count on her, knowing I can be my full self, knowing that she has cheered the loudest on my journey, giving me my flowers, being my support when I feel frustrated and broken, I can't explain the unconditional love I feel for my sister.

We have taken to refusing to add "in-law" to our titles because we have become true sisters. All the family trips and life's experiences, ups and downs, having her by my side has been a foundational blessing as has the example of how powerful it is when someone simply shows up time and time again.

I witness her today being the best mother to my nieces and nephew, having bonds with them we both could not have imagined as kids ourselves. Her door is always open to anyone, especially a child in need. She has been a safe haven and harbor for many, including my heart and my child.

What Valencia taught me is that family isn't just about blood; it's about choice, commitment, and consistency. She chose to move beyond our rocky beginning. She chose to see past our early misunderstandings. She chose to love not just me but my daughter as if we were her own blood.

The transformation of our relationship from tension to sisterhood didn't happen overnight. It required both of us to soften our hearts, check our egos, and recognize that we were fighting for the same things: to be good mothers, to provide for our children, to overcome our own traumas, and to create something better for the next generation.

When I think about the specific ways Valencia has shown up for my daughter, my heart overflows with gratitude. She has been there during moments when I couldn't be, providing the kind of love and support that you can't pay for, can't ask for, and can't repay. She has loved my child when that child needed love most, without condition, without question, without hesitation.

That kind of love that shows up when no one else does, that stays consistent through life's ups and downs, that chooses you again and again is the rarest and most precious gift in this world.

Valencia has shown me what chosen family really means. She has proven that the strongest bonds aren't always the ones we're born with, but often the ones we choose to nurture, protect, and honor. She has taught me that sisterhood isn't about blood; it's about heart.

In a world where relationships often fade with distance, time, or changing circumstances, Valencia and I have built something unbreakable. We've weathered the storms of young adulthood, early parenthood, career changes, family dynamics, and personal growth. And we emerged not just intact, but stronger.

She has been my safe space when the world felt unsafe, my cheerleader when I doubted myself, my partner in the beautiful chaos of raising children, and my sister in every way that matters.

Valencia was extraordinary in the most ordinary way simply by choosing love over conflict, consistency over convenience, and sisterhood over separation. She took a relationship that could have remained strained and rocky and transformed it into one of the most foundational bonds of my life.

She revealed that sometimes the most important family members are the ones who choose to love you, who earn their place in your heart through their actions, who prove their commitment through their consistency.

The way she has loved my daughter, the way she has shown up for our family, the way she has transformed from competitor to collaborator to sister  all of it represents the power of growth, forgiveness, and chosen love.

She didn't have to become my sister. She chose to. And that choice, renewed every day for over a decade, has become one of the most beautiful and unbreakable bonds of my life.

That's what extraordinary ordinary women do; they choose love, they are present consistently, and they prove that the family we choose can be just as strong, just as meaningful, and just as foundational as the family we're born into.

Thank you, Valencia, V, my sister, Auntie V, for your resilience, for your will to keep going, for all you sacrifice for your kids and all those around you. Sister, remember how special you are, how important you are as an extraordinary

ordinary woman. All your hopes and dreams matter, and I wish them all to come true.

Thank you, sister. Love you to life in this life and the next.

You are my sister of the heart, and I am grateful every day that life brought us together, that we chose to grow beyond our rocky beginning, and that we built something beautiful and unbreakable in its place.

# *Special Recognition*:
## More Extraordinary Ordinary Women

While the women featured in the previous chapters received full tributes, there are so many more extraordinary ordinary women who have touched my life, believed in my potential, and contributed to my journey. Each deserves recognition for the ways they lifted me, supported me, or simply taught me what it means to live with grace, strength, and love.

---

**Angelique** - My best friend's mother who loved me like her own daughter, which meant holding me to the same high standards of accountability and respect she expected from her children. The Bible she gave me became my anchor when I returned to school as an adult at Cornerstone Christian University, a tangible reminder that with faith and determination, all things are possible.

147

**Holly Sharp** - From tenth grade, she carried a five-star planner and wrote down every goal, plan, and dream for her future, then methodically achieved them all and more. Even as a cancer survivor, she continues to approach each day with intention and purpose, planning and scheduling to ensure she extracts every ounce of possibility from this life— a true inspiration for living with vision and determination.

**Dolly, Bridgette, and Nichole Sallie** - When I was a twenty-one-year-old pregnant girl with no home and no job, you welcomed me into your lives simply because I was dating your cousin, giving me a place to live and feeding me when I was in need. Your gift of joy and laughter during one of my most lost and vulnerable times will forever hold a place dear in my heart. You are a truly extraordinary woman who showed love to a stranger who became family.

**Susan Teacher at GRCC**- My first class returning to college as an adult mother, you were an immediate light when I was nervous and uncertain about my abilities. You taught me to show the audience rather than just tell them, and you were the first person to plant the seed that would eventually bloom into this book when you said, "You should be a writer."

**Denise** - A woman who walks the walk of faith and love, you not only trained, helped hire, and took a chance on a

148

young pregnant medical assistant, but became a mentor and living example of how to treat every individual with genuine love and compassion. Your laughter and light still fill my heart. When we reunited after almost a decade and you said "I love you, sister," you meant it, and I love you too, Denise.

**Eileen** - You encouraged me to go back and get my degree when my daughter was still young, telling me "You have so much potential - do it now while she is young, it's better." Although I didn't yet believe in myself then, but several years later, I took your advice and transformed my entire career trajectory. You were a true inspiration. Thank you for your friendship and encouragement that planted seeds for my future.

**Carmen** - Your unwavering work ethic, deep love for your family, and refreshingly pragmatic approach to life taught me what it means to consistently do the right thing, even when it's hard. Those funny lunchtime stories that carried me through long, challenging workdays were more than entertainment; they were lifelines of joy and connection that reminded me friendship can flourish even in the most demanding environments.

**Elizabeth** - The kindest, most compassionate healthcare provider I ever had the privilege to work alongside, your playful spirit brought joy to our patient care through fun nicknames like "Mandible" and "Mandarian" that still make me smile. When fate brought us together years later at the hospital where my grandmother was dying, you became my angel, patiently explaining her labs, gently preparing me for what was to come, and offering the comfort that only someone with your extraordinary heart could provide during one of life's most sacred and difficult moments.

**Sharon** - Part of our cherished lunchtime crew with Carmen, you created a sacred space where three mothers and women could share the real stories of trying to make it in the world—the struggles, the victories, the daily challenges of balancing it all. Your infectious sense of humor and genuine friendship became the bright spot in many difficult days, reminding me that laughter and sisterhood can carry us through anything life throws our way.

**Amy** - When I was a struggling young mother and you were a college student, we discovered a friendship that transcended our different life stages through your extraordinary heart for others. Your quiet intelligence and boundless compassion transformed every patient interaction from the moment they walked through the door, and there wasn't an animal you wouldn't stop to rescue or a child your heart wouldn't break to help. The countless times you took me to lunch when money was tight, and the honor of having you stand beside me at my wedding, helped me understand what selfless friendship looks like.. People who are blessed to have you in their lives have found a rare treasure of kindness and love.

**Divya** - We started together as new analysts — you fresh out of college and me a young mom about to get married — and you became my window into the beautiful richness of your culture and traditions. Through our conversations about marriage, love, and life, you expanded my worldview and showed me different perspectives on what commitment and partnership could look like, and being able to virtually attend your Indian wedding was a privilege that deepened my appreciation for our friendship and the learning we shared together.

**Ann Marie** - Affectionately known as AML, every time I run into you or we get a chance to chat, it's like no time has passed at all. Being your colleague and friend was such a privilege, and I will never forget how we survived those long work hours and drives together with laughter until our faces hurt — the kind of genuine joy that made even the most challenging days bearable. Always rooting for you, friend.

**Heidi** - The amount of joy you brought me during my early days of becoming an analyst and learning that world is indescribable. I can still picture us in tears after intense team meetings, using "jabber" to try and "take each other down" in playful rounds of making each other laugh via instant message. You have the best heart and are one of the finest people I ever had the privilege to know, turning what could have been overwhelming learning experiences into moments of pure joy and connection.

**Amanda** - Hutch! An amazing colleague who became a treasured friend during those intense analyst years of implementation life, when long hours and high-pressure projects forged unbreakable bonds. Years later, receiving that LinkedIn message from you saying it was cool to see where my career had progressed meant the world to me — proof that true workplace friendships transcend job changes and time, and that the best colleagues become lifelong cheerleaders for each other's success.

**Jill** - Where do I begin? You are an exceptional daughter, wife, mother, friend, colleague, and all-around human being whose depth and authenticity made every conversation meaningful. Working alongside you was an honor. Through those deep conversations about raising our kids, advancing our careers, and navigating everything life threw at us, we became more than colleagues; we became soul sisters who got each other through hard days and celebrated every victory together. Thank you doesn't seem enough for a bond that transcends time and distance. No matter how much time passes, you and I are connected always. Love you, friend.

**Meghan**- Madge! From the first day you sat at a cubicle near mine, we became fast friends with an instant understanding that allowed us to be honest, transparent, and authentic from the very start. Over a decade of friendship, we've witnessed each other through so much of life's journey — the triumphs, the challenges, the growth, and the transformation. I'm grateful we've stayed connected through it all, and I'm absolutely thrilled to be watching you live your best life in this beautiful second act, manifesting nothing but love, light, and joy for all that's ahead.

**Jessica** - Jess! I had the honor of onboarding you as a new analyst straight out of college, and what a privilege it was to work side by side as I watched you find your career rhythm and blossom into the incredible professional you've become. Witnessing your growth both personally and professionally and seeing you evolve into an amazing wife and mother have been pure joy. Everyone who knows you is so lucky to have your light in their lives, and I miss you tremendously! Sending you all my love, always.

**Camellia** - To my dearest mother-in-law, you have been the embodiment of unconditional family love, providing shelter through countless storms and unwavering support through all of life's seasons. The extraordinary bond you share with Mariona is one of this lifetime's most precious gifts. Watching you love and guide her has filled my heart beyond measure. I celebrate not only the remarkable woman you are, but all you have overcome with such grace and strength, and the way you consistently show up for your family with a love that knows no bounds. You hold a treasured place in my heart for all eternity.

**Nicole**- From the moment I met you, I was in awe of your intelligence, work ethic, and unwavering dedication to being the most wonderful person, wife, and mother. Watching you support your husband through medical school while taking our little Gray Bug with you on work travels and beyond exemplifies what true partnership and resilience look like. I am honored to call you friend and want you to know that no matter where you are in the world, I am cheering for you the loudest and will always be here if you need me. You are truly a remarkable woman who deserves the world.

**Natalia**- I had the privilege of meeting you in 2020 during a tough year and an even tougher implementation, but from our very first conversation, we bonded and formed an instant sisterhood that became one of the bright lights in those challenging times. Your camaraderie, infectious laughter, wise family advice, and authentic friendship have been lifelines that carried me through some of the most difficult days, reminding me that even in the hardest circumstances, genuine connections can bloom and flourish. You are truly a remarkable woman, and I am always rooting for you, always here for you. Love you always, friend.

**Barb** - The first IT Director I worked with when I became an analyst, you were an astute woman who navigated tough waters in an industry full of male counterparts with unwavering professionalism and strategic thinking. Your matter-of-fact approach always cut straight to the truth: "You will grow, but at some point you will need a degree, so go after it." Before your well-planned and strategic retirement, you sent me a note reminding me to go for it. And I did, Barb. Your direct wisdom and belief in my potential became the catalyst for my educational journey and every opportunity that followed.

**Anna** - An incredible woman who has defied extraordinary circumstances and weathered life-altering storms with a grace and strength that leaves me in awe. Watching you navigate health battles while maintaining your commitment as a career-driven wife and mother of two boys has shown me what true resilience looks like. You don't just survive the challenges life throws at you, you rise above them and continue to shine. My deepest admiration goes to you, sister, for proving that strength isn't just about enduring hardship, but about thriving despite it.

**Miah** - My dearest Miah Friah, I was privileged to become your aunt when you were just four years old, and being your TT Mandy has been one of the greatest honors of my life. I've had the joy of walking alongside you, witnessing a curly-haired cutie blossom into a resilient young woman with such extraordinary gifts and boundless potential. I am always right here cheering for you, ready for those good life check-in phone conversations, and every time we get together lights up my heart more than you'll ever know. There are no limits in this world, Miah. Keep dreaming as big as your beautiful heart can imagine, now and always.

**Makaila** - Kay Kay, I have been blessed to witness your growth from your earliest moments in this world, and watching you flourish into the remarkable young woman you are today continues to amaze me. Your strength, humor, drive, heart, and ambitious goals as you approach eighteen fill me with such pride and excitement for your future. Please know that I will be here for you always, right by your side for any questions, support, or simply just to talk, you can count on me without hesitation. I am SO proud to be your TT and will be rooting for you every step of the way. Not even the sky is the limit, Kay. Let no one put you in a box ever, because this world is yours for the taking, baby girl. Go get it all.

**Maliyah**- Maliyah Jordyn, my treasured dinner date who brings such joy to every moment we share! You stole my heart from the very moment you entered this world and took it by storm (quite literally), radiating the purest essence of love and light that touches everyone around you. As the baby of our family, you possess this magical ability to connect hearts and bring people together. Every single person who knows you falls completely under the spell of your extraordinary spirit. While the world sees a sweet, sensitive young girl with the biggest heart, I see so much more: a strong, fierce soul burning bright with all the ingredients needed to transform this world in beautiful ways. I am beyond blessed to be your TT, to witness your growth, to learn from your wisdom, and to serve as your biggest cheerleader, friend, and mentor whenever you need me. As our special song reminds us, "You can count on me like 1-2-3, I'll be there" always and forever. I cannot wait to watch you shine your brilliant light and see what incredible path you choose in this lifetime, because I know with absolute certainty that you will touch countless lives with that magnificent heart of yours.

**Sydnee**- Syd! Watching you transform into the remarkable young woman you are today has been one of life's greatest privileges. You are the living definition of an overcomer and survivor and seeing you not just surviving but absolutely thriving at college as a D-1 athlete while finding your unique

157

place in this world fills my heart to overflowing. Your journey from challenges to triumph shows the incredible strength and determination that lives within you. I am here for you always, cheering from the sidelines, celebrating every victory, and ready with support whenever you need me. Please know that there is NO dream too big for your extraordinary spirit, and all good things in this world are meant for you. You deserve boundless love, endless hope, and all the happiness this beautiful life has to offer.

**Tonya** - Aunt Tonya, my favorite aunt growing up who created the most cherished childhood memories with your enormous heart and boundless generosity. I remember when we were a young, struggling family and you arrived without hesitation, filling our cupboards with food and taking Mariona and me to fun events that brought such joy to our lives. Your example of selfless giving has stayed with me always, and I am forever grateful that you blessed the world with one of its most beautiful gifts: Sydnee. I will never forget your kindness and love, and I hope to exemplify that same spirit of generosity in my own life today.

**Dr. Gloria** - Dr. Gloria! When you reached out to me on LinkedIn and offered me the opportunity to be interviewed on my first podcast, I was both nervous and exhilarated by the chance to share my story on such a meaningful platform. Getting to know you and learning about your own remarkable journey of resilience has profoundly inspired me to push beyond self-imposed boundaries and limiting beliefs that once held me back. Your willingness to amplify other women's voices and create spaces for authentic storytelling is a testament to your generous spirit and commitment to lifting others. Thank you for giving me that transformative opportunity and for being such a powerful source of inspiration in my life.

**Dora**- Dora, my sweet niece and twin spirit, there has been a special joy and profound connection between us from the very moment I first held you in my arms. "Proud" doesn't begin to capture how I feel witnessing your transformation into the remarkable young woman you've become. Watching you overcome life's obstacles and pain, persevering through every challenge, and reaching for your dreams with such bold determination fills my heart beyond measure. You and I share a heart and mind for so many things, and one of my most treasured memories will always be sharing the ocean with you for the first time as we explored and snorkeled through the clearest waters in this remarkable world together. I am deeply grateful to be part of your journey and to witness your incredible strength. All the joy, all the good things, all the beautiful possibilities this world has to offer. You truly deserve each and every one, today and always.

**Hailee**- Ms. Hailee, you are the one who started it all the one who made me Auntie Mandy for the very first time and opened my heart to a love I never knew existed. Seeing you now as a wife and mother fills my heart with overwhelming joy, watching you flourish in roles that seem custom-made for your nurturing spirit and generous heart. And now you have blessed me with another incredible gift: your beautiful little girl Vivian, making me a great aunt and adding yet another layer of love to our family bond. I want you to know how deeply I love you and how many people are praying for you and rooting for you to experience all the magnificent love and happiness this life has to offer. You deserve every beautiful blessing, baby girl, and I am always here whenever you need me.

**Rosenda**- Chany! My sweet sister-in-law, you have been a cherished part of my life now longer than not, which means there is hardly a family memory, holiday, birthday celebration with the kids growing up, or special occasion that doesn't hold you in a treasured place in my heart. Having a sister of such incredible strength who loves her family with such fierce devotion and has put up with my brother for so many years is no small feat (sorry, bro!). Your unwavering loyalty, your generous spirit, and your ability to keep our family grounded and connected through every season of life has been a blessing beyond measure. Thank you for being such an amazing sister-in-law to walk alongside in this beautiful, chaotic journey we call life.

**Roxy** - Roxy Girl! Our friendship journey began when I started seeing you to keep my hair from showing my age, but what I discovered was so much more precious than perfect color. You are an incredible woman of strength and resilience who loves her children fiercely and dedicates herself to making everyone around her feel beautiful and empowered to tackle whatever life throws their way. Your chair isn't just a place for hair transformations; it's a sanctuary where women leave feeling more confident, more valued, and more ready to take on the world. I am forever grateful for our connection and the way you've enriched my life beyond just keeping me looking fabulous. And I promise, not another soul will touch my hair. You're stuck with me, Roxy Girl!

**Donna** - Momma Donna, I want you to know that you are celebrated and that I am deeply honored to know you as a living inspiration of what motherhood truly means. Your selfless dedication to your family and the way you pour your heart into loving and supporting everyone around you embodies everything anyone could envision when they think of a wonderful, devoted mother. I want you to know that people see your beautiful example and are inspired by the way you change the world for the better simply by loving,

161

supporting, and encouraging all those in your orbit with such genuine care. Momma Donna, you are an absolute gem whose impact reaches far beyond what you may ever realize.

**Inez**- Inez, I had the privilege of being your colleague at Trinity Health, where I witnessed you being a supervisor who truly cared for the people who reported to you. As a woman who took such devoted care of her family while overcoming significant personal pain and circumstances, you pushed forward with remarkable strength to care for your grandson and family. I was deeply inspired by your resilience and boundless love. I want you to know how extraordinary ordinary you are, proving that sometimes the most profound acts of courage happen quietly, in the daily choice to keep loving and leading despite life's challenges.

**Gabriella** - Gabriella, I had the privilege to work with you as consultants and felt a kindred spirit with you right away! As a young woman in her twenties, I was blown away by what you have accomplished and experienced in this lifetime. The way you were able to encourage me and see me as a leader and mentor was such an honor to experience and your belief in my potential meant more than you know. Gabriella, I am always your champion because your compassion for others and the way you see the world gives me such hope for the future. I am so grateful to have met you and to witness the incredible impact you're making at such a young age. You will always have a friend in me, and I cannot wait to see all the amazing things you'll continue to accomplish.

**Chelsea** - Chelsea, you are truly one of the hardest working, most strategic and intelligent young women I have ever met. You inspire me to keep pushing, keep challenging myself, and to have hope for the future by witnessing you grow and lead in real time with such purpose and vision. Your dedication to excellence and your ability to think strategically while maintaining your authenticity sets you apart in remarkable ways. I plan to see your name in big-time spaces because I know your talent and work ethic will take you there, and I am honored to be in your network and to call you friend.

**Amy H.** - Amy, you opened your gym to me and welcomed me as your trainee, inviting me to join a remarkable group of women bonded not just by moving our bodies to stay healthy, but by being in genuine community with one another as we navigated work, life, marriage, and children's milestones and challenges along the way. You came into my life at a time when I desperately needed community with other women, a space to learn, grow, and lead alongside others who understood the beautiful complexity of balancing it all. Thank you for creating that sacred space for me, for being an exceptional trainer who saw fitness as more than just physical transformation, and for welcoming me into your world with such warmth. I pray life is treating you and your family with all the abundant blessings you deserve, because you've sowed so much goodness into so many lives, and I am deeply grateful to be among that blessed group.

**Lexi Marie** - Lexi, my bonus daughter, I am so grateful to be your bonus mom and to witness the woman you are becoming. Watching you set your goals and work toward accomplishing them shows me your determination and focus. Keep moving forward and doing all the right things as you create a positive example for your baby girl to follow. Keep dreaming big because you truly can achieve great things, and I am here to support and encourage you every step of the way on your journey.

**Sarah** - Sarah, my treasured childhood friend who shares some of my most cherished memories from those carefree days when we were mischievous little kids dreaming of helping animals and taking over the world together. The countless hours I spent with your family and running around the neighborhood as children will always hold a special place in my heart. Those golden days of pure friendship and boundless imagination. Now here we are, both holding master's degrees from MSU (Uncle Gill no doubt is beaming with pride), and we're both fulfilling those childhood dreams of helping people while still loving animals with the same fierce devotion. I'm certain you are an incredible wife and mother, having learned from such a shining example in your own family, and you were always the most caring big sister to your siblings. Thank you for all those beautiful childhood memories that shaped who I became, and know that I am cheering for you always, wishing all the love, joy, and continued success to you and your beautiful family.

**Becky**- Becky, beloved mother to Sarah, Laura, and Erin, I remember the devastating phone call from Sarah after I had moved over an hour away, learning the heartbreaking news that you had passed away. You were a beautiful woman who battled cancer with incredible bravery and grace, though you would ultimately lose that courageous fight. You welcomed me into your home with open arms, treated me like one of your own daughters, and embodied the epitome of class, grace, compassion, and everything anyone would want a mother to be. Becky, you would be so immensely proud of your girls today. They are remarkable, resilient, strong, and devoted to their families, reflecting the incredible foundation of love and values you gave them. Thank you for the precious love and memories you shared with me during those formative years. You are truly missed and your legacy lives on beautifully in the extraordinary women you raised.

Each of these women represents a moment of connection, kindness, guidance, or inspiration that contributed to the tapestry of my life. While their stories may not fill chapters, their impact fills my heart with gratitude for the countless ways women lift other women, often without even knowing the profound difference they make.

**Damita:** My dear sister, you have always been the epitome of grace, patience, and compassion. Every time I am with you, you radiate the most beautiful energy of love and embody what it means to be a gracious hostess, extending such warmth to your family and all those around you. You are a true example of unconditional love.

**Victoria:** My Estie Bestie, I am so grateful the divine brought you into my life. Your story of overcoming adversity with resilience, triumph, and love is one that I cherish and that inspires me every day. I cannot wait until the world hears and is inspired by all you have accomplished. Thank you for being the keeper of my beauty so my heart can shine outwardly. I pray pure blessings over you and your loved ones.

**Destiny** — I am so grateful to have watched you grow into the incredible young woman you are today. Having you in our lives as a chosen family member fills every moment with joy, laughter, and love. You are worthy of every good thing this life has to offer. Everything your heart desires is within reach, trust that you are right on time, keep moving forward, and never forget how deeply you are loved.

**To All the Women I Have Yet to Meet** - I can't wait to get to know you! I am already filled with gratitude for the many, many women who will come into my life, whose stories will change me, inspire me, and encourage me to be the very best version of myself. I already love you and that I am hoping to encourage you too. Let's build this world together, being extraordinary and ordinary side by side, lifting each other as we climb, and creating ripples of love and possibility that extend far beyond what we can imagine. Thank you in advance for the light you will bring to my life and the lives of countless others. I love you already, and I cannot wait to witness the incredible ways you will change the world simply by being yourselves.

**Five generations**

# About The Author

**Mandy K. Crosby** is a brand strategist, healthcare consultant, and advocate for women in leadership who has built her career on the foundation of one powerful truth: we rise by lifting others.

From her early days as a young mother at 22 navigating the challenges of starting over, through her journey in healthcare and eventual transition into the world of startups and venture capital, she has been shaped by extraordinary ordinary women who saw her potential before she could see it herself. Today, she pays that gift forward as a mentor, leader, and champion for emerging founders and women leaders across all industries.

As a healthcare consultant and the Global Head of Branding for a tech startup, she helps innovative companies craft compelling narratives and build brands that resonate. Her work spans from early-stage startups to established enterprises, always with a focus on authentic storytelling and strategic positioning. She brings a unique perspective informed by her diverse background in healthcare, business development, and brand strategy.

Beyond her professional work, she is passionate about creating opportunities for the next generation of women leaders. She believes that the most powerful force in any woman's life is another woman who believes in her potential and refuses to let her waste it.

*Extraordinary Ordinary Women* is her debut book. A love letter to the women who lifted her and an invitation to readers to recognize and become the extraordinary ordinary women in their own circles.

She lives in Michigan with her husband as empty nesters, where she continues to lift while she climbs.

*If this book has touched you in a meaningful way, please take a moment and write a review. It's the best way to help others find it.*

*Thank you for your support.*

www.ingramcontent.com/pod-product-compliance
Lightning Source LLC
Chambersburg PA
CBHW070920130626
46555CB00001B/218